HOW TO KNOW GOD'S VOICE
IN HIS PRESENCE

STUDY GUIDE

Rev. 10/22

ACKNOWLEDGMENTS

ZOE Ministries International is dedicated to training, equipping and sending believers into the world to minister by the leading of the Holy Spirit. This ministry helps build the body of Christ and encourages God's people to use their gifts and talents for His glory. It is for this purpose that this publication has been compiled by the leading of the Holy Spirit and the input of many people. ZOE Ministries wishes to thank them for their support, time, and talents in contributing to this handout packet. We give our Lord all the praise and glory for this work!

CONTENTS

COURSE OUTLINE

Lesson 1   **INTRODUCTION—MAN'S FALL AND SEPARATION FROM GOD**
Class Articles: *Dual Status,* J. Buckingham
The Boy With The Shining Face, C. Marshall
A Tender Heart Before The Lord, K. Henry
The River Of God's Pleasure, F. Frangipane

Lesson 2   **BEING LOOSED!**
Scripture: **John 11**
Assigned Article: *Manipulation, Control And Fear Of Man,* J. Meyer

Lesson 3   **UNTIE THE COLT; THE LORD HAS NEED OF IT!**
Scripture: **Luke 19:28–40; Matthew 21:1–11; Mark 11:1–11; John 12:9–19**
Frangipane: Introduction and Chapter 1
Assigned Article: *The Glory Of The Upper Room,* C. Freidzon

Lesson 4   **JESUS—OUR PASSOVER LAMB**
Scripture: **Matthew 26:1–5; Exodus 12:1–28**
Frangipane: Chapters 2 and 3
Study Help: "The Lamb Of God" ZOE Ministries
Assigned Articles: *God So Loved The World,* J. Cornwall
Why The Cross?, R. Vander Laan
Supplementary Reading: *The Power Of Jesus' Blood,* D. Kuhn

Lesson 5   **BETRAYAL VERSES LOVE**
Scripture: **Matthew 26:6–35; Mark 14:3–26**
Frangipane: Chapters 4, 5 and 6
Assigned Article: *The Truth About Judas—Betrayer Of Christ,* D. Wilkerson

Lesson 6   **DECISIONS—STAGE ONE**
Scripture: **Matthew 26:36–56; Mark 14:32–50; Luke 22:39–53**
Frangipane: Chapters 7 and 8
Assigned Article: *Our First Priority,* H. Schroeder

Lesson 7   **HUMILIATION—STAGE TWO**
Scripture: **Matthew 26:57–75; Luke 22:54–65; John 18:12–27**
Frangipane: Chapters 9 and 10
Assigned Articles: *Fill Us With Your Passion, Lord!,* K. Henry
Psalm 77—Are You Listening, God?, J. Stocker

Lesson 8   **OUR CHOICE—STAGES THREE AND FOUR**

Scripture:	**Matthew 27:1–26; Mark 15:1–15;**
	Luke 22:66—23:25; John 18:28–19:1
Frangipane:	Chapters 11 and 12
Assigned Articles:	*Is God Opposing The Church?*, F. Frangipane
	The Marvelous Benefits Of Repentance!, D. Wilkerson

Lesson 9   **THE ROBE, THE CROWN AND THE CROSS—STAGES FIVE AND SIX**

Scripture:	**Matthew 27:27–32; Mark 15:16–21**
Frangipane:	Chapters 13 and 14
Assigned Articles:	*The Calling Of Separation*, D. Lindsay
	Learning Humility From Jesus, R. Hufton

Lesson 10   **CARRYING THE CROSS—STAGES SEVEN AND EIGHT**

Scripture:	**Matthew 27:32–44; Mark 8:34–38; Mark 15:21–32;**
	Luke 23:26–43; John 19:17–27
Frangipane:	Chapters 15, 16 and 17
Assigned Articles:	*Jesus Christ Is Great*, P. Lowenberg
	How To See God Clearly, B. Weis

Lesson 11   **DEPARTURE FROM HIS PRESENCE—STAGES NINE AND TEN**

Scripture:	**Matthew 27:45–50; John 19:28–30; Psalm 139:7–8;**
	Jeremiah 23:24; Deuteronomy 30:11–20
Frangipane:	Chapters 18 and 19
Assigned Articles:	*Wrestling With God*, J. Buckingham
	Guard Your Affection For Christ!, D. Wilkerson
	Making A Habitation For The Lord, D. Ravenhill

Lesson 12   **PAST THE VEIL AND INTO HIS PRESENCE**

Scripture:	**Exodus 26:31–33; Matthew 27:50–54;**
	Hebrews 9:3, 7–14; 10:19–22
Frangipane:	Chapters 22, 21, 22 and Closing
Assigned Articles:	*Seven Women Lay Hold Of One Man*, D. Wilkerson
	Eye Hath Not Seen Nor Ear Heard..., U.S. Grant

Appendix   "Jesus and the Feast of the Passover" ZOE Ministries

Study Materials:
1. Bible, any version.
2. *Holiness, Truth and the Presence of God*, Francis Frangipane, Arrow Publications, Cedar Rapids, Iowa, USA, 1986.
3. Various Articles in the Study Guide:
   a. Class Article—to be read in class
   b. Assigned Article—to be read in preparation for class
   c. Study Help—for the participant's use in studying at home
   d. Supplementary Reading—optional—will not be discussed in class

FOREWORD

Dear Participant,

In **Revelation 2:4** Jesus speaks to the church at Ephesus, telling them that they have forsaken their first love for Him. How easy it is to allow the cares of the world to slip into our lives and replace that "first love" we had when we first accepted Jesus as our Lord.

This course, *In His Presence*, brings us once again to the cross and the significant part it plays in our lives. We take an intense look at the last week of Jesus' life, examining how He laid down His life so that we might have eternal life.

Like all the courses in ZOE's "Knowing" series, this course causes us to fall deeper in love with our Lord Jesus. It is His desire that daily we walk in close communion with Him, and that we are familiar with not only His deeds, but His ways as well.

This is truly a soul-searching course designed for people who have an understanding of the character of God and His love for us. We know that this course will change your life—as it truly impacted ours! We pray that the Holy Spirit will refresh and renew a deep love for Jesus in your heart and in the hearts of all the class members.

Enjoy!

In His service,

Dick and Ginny Chanda
Founding Directors

A NOTE TO COURSE PARTICIPANTS

What ZOE Is!

1. A ministry that provides training for disciple-making.
2. Participatory classes where all are encouraged to share and contribute.
3. A situation where the leader (facilitator) decreases and the participants increase.
4. A drawing out of ministry gifts and preparation for the Lord's calling on individual lives.
5. A time when one can grow in the understanding and appreciation of others' gifts.
6. A safe environment in which an individual can feel comfortable to practice operating in his or her gifts.
7. A time of understanding the heart of the Father and applying that to one's life.

What ZOE Is Not!

1. A traditional Bible study.
2. A class where the leader speaks and the people take notes.
3. A place where people can air their opinions or gripes.
4. A place where people can discuss church doctrines.
5. A time when "weird" ministry happens.

A Reminder to ZOE Participants:

"A ZOE course is not just a Bible study; our leader is a facilitator and coach, not a teacher."

It is our desire that the Lord Jesus Christ be glorified in all that is said and done in ZOE classes.
We wish to foster an understanding of the operation of His Holy Spirit and to yield to His workings.

MAIN PRINCIPLES

Lesson 1: Mankind has been separated from God because of our sin, but from the beginning God made provision to restore the fellowship He so desires to have with us. It is through Jesus' sacrifice and shedding of His blood that we can be in right standing with God, enter into God's presence with confidence, and have fellowship with Him.

Lesson 2: If we are in any kind of bondage, our understanding of the principles laid down for us by Jesus may be hindered. We need to ask the Holy Spirit to begin to unwrap for us any areas in which we are bound.

Lesson 3: God has chosen to use people to fulfill His plans and purposes on earth. The Lord wants us loosed from anything holding us in bondage so that we can be free to do what He needs us to do.

Lesson 4: We can come to God only because of the atoning work of Christ, our Passover Lamb. As His blood covers us by faith, we can abide in God's glory.

Lesson 5: God wants us to extend extravagant love toward Jesus. Are we willing to give to Jesus anything He asks us of us because He laid down His life for us? Are we willing to lay down our own plans and ambitions for Him? Are we willing to show our love for Jesus despite what people will think?

Lesson 6: As we see Jesus pray in anguish in the Garden of Gethsemane and allow Himself to be arrested, we need to decide if we are willing to follow in Jesus' footsteps. Are we willing to follow Jesus and put our relationship with the Father first in our lives, even if it means going toward the cross and laying down everything for our Lord?

Lesson 7: As we read of Jesus silently enduring being mocked, spat upon and beaten, we realize that He suffered this humiliation for our sake. He did this so that we would be able to come into the fullness of relationship with Him. Are we willing to stand firm in our belief in Jesus, desire only His approval, and endure humiliation for Him?

Lesson 8: We must choose to avoid pride and hardness of heart and keep our hearts pliable towards the Lord. We need to choose to let go of our sinful attitudes and actions when God reveals them to us. As we truly repent of our sins and turn to Jesus, we will receive the help and forgiveness we need.

Lesson 9: Just as Jesus was stripped of His clothes and His dignity, so we need to be stripped of any idols we have. As God reveals them, we must completely tear down all idols in our lives. Then we can enter into God's presence with hearts free of idolatry.

Lesson 10: Jesus suffered greatly when He was crucified. We need to respond to Jesus' suffering at His crucifixion by choosing to take up our cross and follow Him. We must not be like the Pharisees, who were more concerned with religion than following Jesus.

Lesson 11: We need to understand the significance of Jesus' final words, "It is finished." It was a shout of victory! Jesus won access to God for us because He was willing to take on our sin and be separated from the Father. As we go into God's presence, we go in humility and gratitude, but also in victory.

Lesson 12: We can now enter the Holy of Holies, the presence of God the Father. We do this only through the shed blood of Jesus, which cleanses us from sin. We can go into God's presence with confidence through Jesus, our new and living way.

PARTICIPANT'S RESPONSIBILITIES

I. Course Preparation

A. Read the assigned scriptures and come prepared to share in the course.

1. Ask the Holy Spirit, **"Open my eyes that I may see wonderful things in your law." Psalm 119:18** You may be very familiar with the assigned Scriptures, but the Lord is very faithful and can give you "fresh manna."

2. Look at the Main Principle for the class and apply the Scriptures. Ask yourself the following questions:
   a. How does this Scripture apply to the lesson?
   b. How does this Scripture apply to my life?
   c. What do I need to do to apply this Scripture to my life and to the lives of others for God's glory?

B. Read the assigned chapters or pages in the book and come prepared to share in the course.
Note in your book any thoughts related to the Main Principle for the lesson.

C. Read the assigned articles and come prepared to share in class.
Note any thoughts related to the Main Principle for the lesson.

D. Maintain a journal—a valuable tool in God's hands.
As you learn to hear God's voice and keep a record of His speaking, you will become more aware of what He is saying to you and how He wants to work through you. See the handout "Journaling—A Good Way to Hear God's Voice."

E. Spend time in prayer.
1. Prayer is valuable preparation for these classes. The more time you spend with the Lord, the more you will come to know Him.

2. Spend time with God <u>daily!</u> Avoid crash studying. God shows no partiality—what He has done for others, He will do for you! Growth will come as you respond to God's Holy Spirit at work in your life.

II. Class Participation

A. Training is active! You will be encouraged to **take part in the class discussions and the prayer and ministry time.**

B. You will have the opportunity to **lead the discussion** of the assigned reading as you feel comfortable. No one will be forced to lead—only encouraged!

JOURNALING – A GOOD WAY TO HEAR GOD'S VOICE

What Goes Into a Journal?

1. Your thoughts—impressions, insights, hopes, fears, goals, struggles
2. Your feelings—both positive and negative
3. Your prayers and answers to prayer
4. Excerpts from Scripture and other reading that God seems to be highlighting for you

How To Journal

1. You may choose to use a spiral binder or a hardback blank book, or anything that you can take with you easily on trips.
2. Journal every day, if possible, during the time that you read Scripture and pray. Record in it insights that the Lord gave you that day or the day before.
3. You may want to keep a separate section in your journal for prayers or excerpts from your reading.
4. Write directly to God as if you were talking to Him or writing Him a letter.

The Benefits of Keeping a Journal Are Many

1. Journaling fosters a readiness to hear from God. Personal communion with God takes place as you write out your thoughts and feelings, and record the insights and impressions He gives you.
2. As you read God's Word and record your insights about Scripture, God is faithful to provide the admonitions, encouragement and guidance that you need.
3. Prayers become specific as you place them in print. In addition, God gets the glory when you review your journal and see your prayers have been answered.
4. Journaling helps clarify your thinking. Fears and struggles are more clearly defined so that they can be dealt with.
5. During times of discouragement, it can help to look back over your journal and see God's faithfulness and your progress in spiritual growth.

GUIDELINES FOR LEADING A COURSE DISCUSSION

1. Prayer

As you study the assigned material, ask God for insights. Ask Him to show you the main points to be discussed and questions to ask to aid the discussion. Come a few minutes early to class and pray with the Facilitators before the class begins.

2. Maintain Control of the Discussion

After the class has been turned over to you by the Facilitators, you are to maintain control of the discussion.

    a.   Do not allow one or two participants to dominate the discussion time.

    b.   Stick to the subject. God may give you many insights, but keep the discussion related to the Main Principle of the lesson.

3. Work Within the Allotted Time

For a 2 1/2 hour class:

    Approximately 30 minutes for the book

    Approximately 50 minutes for the Scripture discussion

    Approximately 15 minutes for the articles

        (Allowing 20 minutes for the Facilitators to lead the prayer/ministry)

For a 1 1/2 hour class:

    Approximately 20 minutes for the book

    Approximately 30 minutes for the Scripture discussion

    Approximately 10 minutes for the articles

        (Allowing 10 minutes for the Facilitators to lead the prayer/ministry)

ZOE courses focus on what God says through the Bible. Be careful not to spend too much time on the book or articles, which are provided only as supplements to the Scriptures.

4. Encourage Discussion

Course members should be prepared to share insights that the Lord gave them while they read the assigned material. You may need to draw out these insights by asking questions.

    a.   Begin with a launch question, a broad question that can be answered in a number of different ways by anyone in the group.

    b.   Then use guide questions, which are short questions that keep the discussion moving in a direction that is related to the Main Principle of that lesson. Life application of the principles found in the assigned reading should be a focus during some part of the discussion.

    c.   To close the discussion time, summarize very briefly the main points of the discussion.

May God bless you as you study and pray in preparation for the course. We will be praying for you as you prepare. We love and appreciate you.   *~The Facilitators*

LESSON 1

INTRODUCTION—MAN'S FALL AND SEPARATION FROM GOD

MAIN PRINCIPLE

Mankind has been separated from God because of our sin, but from the beginning God made provision to restore the fellowship He so desires to have with us.
It is through Jesus' sacrifice and shedding of His blood that we can be in right standing with God, enter into God's presence with confidence, and have fellowship with Him.

DISCLAIMER

The articles that follow have been chosen to give you, the reader, a broader perspective on many of the issues presented in the course. All the ideas in these articles do not necessarily represent the views of *ZOE Ministries International*. However, we pray that as you read and study, you will glean a sense of what is in the author's heart. At all times we need to ask the question, "Does this line up with the Word of God?"

DUAL STATUS

by Jamie Buckingham

THOSE OF US WHO HAVE TASTED FROM THE SPRING OF INTIMACY WITH GOD WILL NEVER AGAIN BE SATISFIED WITH LAPPING FROM EARTH'S POLLUTED PUDDLES.

A growing number of us, I have discovered, have tasted heaven but returned to (or remained on) earth. We are the ones who have literally "entered into His presence."

Some have experienced that wonderful level of intimacy with God through prayer and revelation. Others, like myself, have been forced upward—out of carnality and selfish living—through personal crises. Some have actually died—or come close to it—and returned like Lazarus from that marvelous place of peace to a world in turmoil.

All of us are confused about our dual status: one foot in heaven and another on earth.

We all experience, as I am still experiencing, the problem of re-entry into "life as usual." We are different. Not like other people. We will always be that way. Having tasted from the sweet spring of intimacy with God, we will never again be satisfied with lapping from Earth's polluted puddles.

In Revelation 2:4–5, the risen Christ chided the pastor at Ephesus for having lost his first love. He told him: "Remember therefore from where you have fallen; repent and do the first works, or else I will come to you quickly and remove your lampstand from its place—unless you repent" (v. 5, NKJV).

We all need, on occasion, to stop and remember what our "first love" was like. We need to recall that overpowering rush of emotion that we now smile and call "puppy love."

I couldn't eat for thinking of her. I'd sneak away, find a phone and talk with her for hours about nothing. Those long nights, lying in bed looking at the ceiling—longing, dreaming. Oh, how I wanted to be with her. I'd rush off to school early to meet her in the parking lot. Just a smile, the touch of her hand, the smell of her perfume would set my heart wildly beating. Nothing mattered: father or mother, studies, sports—all faded into insignificance when I thought of her.

And I was only in the seventh grade.

So it is with those of us who have been to heaven's gate, have heard the sound of His voice, have felt the touch of His saving, healing hand. Nothing else—no love, no desire, no pleasure—will ever match His sweet, holy presence.

In 2 Corinthians 12, Paul described it as being "caught up to the third heaven." But to keep him from becoming conceited, God allowed a "thorn in the flesh"—a companion of pain—to accompany him on earth and

February 1992, Charisma

be with him until his final return. Thorns, it seems, always accompany visits to glory. No one who has walked in His presence will ever be allowed to strut.

Don't regret the limp. Only fear that you lose that wonderful intimacy that came when life was so helpless and death so close.

Francis Frangipane once told me of the beginning of his little church in Cedar Rapids, Iowa. A spiritual idealist, he committed himself to spend every morning—all morning—in prayer. Then his church grew. (Churches with praying pastors always grow, it seems.) People with problems began to show up. There weren't enough hours in the day to minister to God and minister to people, too. He cut his prayer time to three hours a day. Then two.

One day, he said, a young friend who had just spent the morning with God stopped by the house. He had a message from God.

"What did God say?"

"God said, 'Tell Francis I miss him.' "

Who among us, having tasted the sweet intimacy of walking with the Father, does not fear those sad words: "I miss you"?

The Bible emphasizes knowing God intimately, as Father. As Daddy.

Jesus often used agricultural terms. Agriculture, in its most basic sense, is not learning how to control the seasons, soils and processes—it's learning how to cooperate with them.

So it is when you've walked with God. Instead of controlling time, you cooperate with time. Instead of controlling people, you cooperate with them. You love with the love of heaven—for you have been there.

Here's my prayer. You can pray it too.

"Lord, keep me aloft without being aloof. Show me how to remain in orbit with you above Earth's poisoned atmosphere, yet dipping at your command to touch, instruct and heal as Jesus did. May I never again be 'of this world.' May I always—in my own mind and in the oft critical eyes of others—belong to a different kingdom. May I be in the world but not of the world, ministering at your pleasure, marching ever to the sound of the different drummer."

Amen.

—Jamie Buckingham devoted his talents and sacrificed his time to teach and spread the gospel, eventually becoming an internationally renowned author, columnist and conference speaker. He was a friend to nearly every significant Christian leader in the charismatic movement until his death in 1992 at the age of 59.

Reprinted by permission *Charisma Magazine* and Strang Communications Company.

THE BOY WITH THE SHINING FACE

by Catherine Marshall

In the Far West of America is an Indian village. Rising out of the desert and towering over the village is a high mountain. Only the very strong can climb it, so all the boys of the village were eager to try.

One day the chief said, "Now, boys, today you may try to climb the mountain. Each of you go as far as you can. When you are too tired to go on, come back. But I want each of you to bring me a twig from the place where you turned back."

Very soon a fat boy came puffing back. In his hand he held out to the chief a cactus leaf. The chief smiled. "My boy, you did not even reach the foot of the mountain. Cactus is a desert flower." Later a second boy returned. He carried a twig of sagebrush. "Well," said the chief, "at least you reached the foot of the mountain."

The next boy to come back had in his hand a cottonwood twig. "Good," said the chief. "You climbed as far as the springs." Another boy came back with some buckthorn. "You, my boy, were really climbing. You were up to the first rocks."

An hour afterward, one boy came back with a branch of pine. To him the chief said, "Good! You made three-quarters of the climb."

The sun was low in the sky when the last boy returned. His hands were empty but his face was shining. He said, "Father, there were no trees where I was. I saw no twigs, but I saw a shining sea."

Now the old chief's face glowed too. "I knew it! When I looked at your face, I knew it…You have been to the top. You needed no twig to tell me. It is written in your eyes. You alone, my boy, have seen the glory and the peace of the mountain."

You know, the very same thing happens to you and me when we have been with our Father in heaven and have talked to Him in prayer and felt His Presence in our hearts. It shows on our faces. It shines in our eyes. We don't have to tell anyone. Other people will see it and know and be glad.

—Catherine Marshall was an author and a wife to Pastor Peter Marshall. Most of her books were collections of her husbands' sermons, as well as his biography *A Man Called Peter*. She also wrote the popular novels titled *Christy* and *Julie*.

A TENDER HEART BEFORE THE LORD

by Kent Henry

Of all the wisdom I have seen and heard through the years, this truth keeps re-appearing: keep a tender heart before the Lord. A tender-hearted person will stay sensitive to the things of God. Maintaining a tender heart before the Lord helps insure a constant flow of spiritual strength and longevity.

Recently while reading the first chapter of the book, *The House of the Lord*, I found a powerful statement. The chapter, written by Francis Frangipane, is entitled "Cleansing the Holy Place."

He states, "…within the psalmist's heart was a dwelling place for the Lord. David was always beholding the Lord (Acts 2:25). Similarly, there is something in our presence, in our spirits, which can be opened or closed to God…the most essential commodity for stimulating revival is a tender, open heart before God."

The Psalmist's Heart

Let us take each point and consider it well. The psalmist heart, what is that? A heart that is set toward God. The heart of a lover always with his love on his heart and mind. A heart possessed by the Lord's person and awesomeness.

Is. 50:7: *For the Lord God helps me, therefore I am not disgraced; therefore, I have set my face like flint, and I know that I shall not be ashamed.* My face is set like flint toward the Lord. I am now affected for the rest of my life, wholly devoted, helplessly addicted to His presence.

So the psalmist's heart was and still is a tender heart before the Lord. The Lord has found His dwelling place in our hearts because we continue to make room for Him there. Then there is an on-going transmission of His presence to us daily as we yield to the Holy Spirit. This is why we are a marked people different from the world.

Always Beholding The Lord

These few words sum up my life's focus and heart ever since I have been saved and Spirit-filled. Beholding the Lord has been a constant thing with me. I guess the understanding of my release from sin and its penalty and the light that flooded my being swept me into the land of "always wanting to behold the Lord." It is some kind of holy, life-changing communion that keeps drawing me, actually wooing me back again and again.

This is the attitude (always beholding the Lord) of a blessed and humble servant. This is the attitude the tender in heart adopt before the Lord that makes them uniquely the friends of God. It keeps them from the place of pride and arrogance. It keeps them in the place of humility and need of God.

Before destruction, the heart of man is haughty, but humility goes before honor (Prov. 18:12).

When you begin to behold the Lord, you will start to understand the realm of His glory. Not just in heaven, but here on earth, there is coming the release of the glory of the Lord. Here is the prayer Jesus prayed.

John 17:24: *Father, I desire that they also, whom Thou hast given Me, be with Me where I am, in order that they may behold my glory, which Thou hast given Me; for Thou didst love Me before the foundation of the world.*

…to behold His glory. What a thought! What a call! What a life—a chosen race, a royal priesthood, a holy nation, a people for God's own possession proclaiming His excellencies and glories (I Pet. 2:9)! This is an honor for his saints, to be such a carrier of His presence. The nations will behold His glory.

A Teachable, Flexible Heart

I began this year with a personal Bible study in the book of Ecclesiastes. This book of the Bible helps me so much because it is a book of reality. Many believers shy away from the book of Ecclesiastes because it seems difficult to understand, but it is a great anchor for hope and life.

Eccl. 4:13: *A poor, yet wise lad is better than an old and foolish king who no longer knows how to receive instruction* (warning). I was flabbergasted when I first read this verse. How could it be possible? How could a king who had been ruling well become foolish and lose the capacity to even hear or receive instruction? The answer is simple—he became unteachable and inflexible in his heart.

The Berkeley translation of Eccl. 4:13, 14 says this: *Better is a youth poor and wise, than a king old and foolish, who no longer knows how to take advice; for the former comes from prison to be king, although in the other's kingdom he was born poor.*

The Taylor Living Bible paraphrase adds a bit more clarity: *It is better to be a poor but wise youth than to be an old and foolish king who refuses all advice. Such a lad could come from prison and succeed. He might even become king, though born in poverty.*

These scriptures are so important to me at this juncture of my life. I am certain that many people are destined to rule over kingdoms they are currently unprepared to handle. I sense the Lord has a true kingly anointing waiting to be released to those who will maintain a tender heart before Him.

You may ask, "What kingdom is at my command? I am not a great decision maker or anybody so famous and important." Remember this. It is not so much what the eyes of men see or think; it is the Lord in heaven who gives value and importance to our calling.

I say, "Rule well over your home and your finances, for the Lord is looking for faithful men and women. Rule well on your job for this is a small kingdom assignment for promotion in the future. Rule well over your prayer and study time in the scriptures for in them you have abundant life. Rule well then over your current affairs and walk with a tender heart before the Lord."

— Kent Henry is a traveling singer and songwriter who teaches and uses praise with prayer and worship and intercession. He is currently also involved in the leadership of Destiny Church of St. Louis.

Reprinted with permission: *Psalmist Magazine*

THE RIVER OF GOD'S PLEASURE

by Francis Frangipane

LET US CONSIDER IT DEEPLY: WE CAN ACTUALLY BRING PLEASURE TO GOD. WHAT AN INCREDIBLE PRIVILEGE.

To His neighbors, Jesus was just a carpenter's son. Yet, before Jesus' public ministry began, before there were any miracles or multitudes, there was a quality in Christ, even when He was a carpenter, that caused God's heart to swell.

From His youth, Jesus' vision for His life was higher than just becoming a good man. His aim reached beyond His commitment to sinless adherence to the Law. The life of Christ was one of focused devotion to His Father.

Thus, Jesus could not have heard a more wondrous utterance than that which God Himself spoke at the Jordan River. At the sound of the Father's voice, the heavens opened and the river of God's pleasure flowed to His son through these words: "You are My beloved Son, in whom I am well pleased" (Mark 1:11, NKJV).

Remember, at this point Jesus was still a "lay person." He had not yet entered public ministry. It was this life as a tradesman offered to God that increased the Father's bliss.

To give God pleasure is the purpose of *our* existence also. Jesus' ability to please the Father while working a non-religious job tells us God is looking for something deeper from us than theology degrees and correct doctrine.

He is looking for our love. And in this, we too can please Him. Whether we are housewives, secretaries or auto mechanics, in God's eyes, true ministry is not in what we do but in what we become to Him.

Jesus said it often: The Father sees in secret (see Matt. 6:4, 6, 18). Amazingly, it is from this very world of the human heart that the gaze of God seeks pleasure. And when He finds a soul who gives, prays, sacrifices or loves purely as an act of worship, the Father finds His own reward for making man.

As the days unfold toward Christ's return, an increasing number of voices will clamor for our attention. There will be church programs and prayer strategies, activities and powerful movements. Signs and wonders will splatter the world, dazzling the mind of man.

In this environment, we must find the place of God's pleasure. We must be intimately acquainted with that in which His soul delights.

Remember too that the days ahead will increase in pressures and troubles. Because iniquity abounds, the love of many will grow cold (see Matt. 24:12). Isn't the world already stricken with this cold love?

Speaking of our world, Paul warns: "But know this, that in the last days perilous times will come: For

February 1995, Charisma

men will be lovers of themselves, lovers of money, boasters, proud, blasphemers, disobedient to parents, unthankful, unholy, unloving, unforgiving, slanderers, without self-control, brutal, despisers of good, traitors, headstrong, haughty, lovers of pleasure rather than lovers of God, having a form of godliness but denying its power" (2 Tim. 3:1-5).

We must not conform to our environment; we must conform to Christ. He always chose to give God pleasure, even amid conflict and cruelty. We too must redeem our confrontations with the irritations and problems of human existence, identifying them as opportunities to give our Father pleasure as we yield our reactions to him.

The fact is that we were not created to live for ourselves but for God. The key to lasting happiness and real pleasure in this world is not found in seeking pleasure but in pleasing Him. And while the Lord desires that we enjoy His gifts and the people He has given us, He wants us to know that we are created first for His pleasure.

"You are worthy, O Lord, to receive glory and honor and power; for You created all things, and by Your will they exist and were created" (Rev. 4:11). Let us consider it deeply: We can actually bring pleasure to God. What an incredible privilege.

Too often, however, we are more aware of the things that *displease* the Lord than of those that *please* Him. We cannot afford to grope blindly through life without knowing what brings pleasure to God.

Let's specifically isolate one way above all others that touches the heart of God. Paul said, "It pleased God... to reveal His Son in me" (Gal. 1:15-16).

The first and most essential pleasure for God is to see His Son revealed in our lives. No one nor any thing brings pleasure to the Father as much as His Son.

Every time we obey Jesus, giving Him access to this world, we please God. Each time Christ forgives or loves or blesses through us, God finds pleasure.

Jesus only did the things He first saw His Father do. Let us also seek God to know how we may reveal Christ in every situation. For in the love between the Father and His Son, the river of God's pleasure flows.

— Francis Frangipane is the founding pastor of River of Life Ministries in Cedar Rapids, Iowa. He has since retired from his pastoral duties. Before retiring he opened an international online school called *In Christ's Image Training* (ICIT).

Reprinted by permission: *Charisma Magazine* and Strang Communications Company.

LESSON 2

INTRODUCTION

MAIN PRINCIPLE

If we are in any kind of bondage, our understanding of the principles laid down for us by Jesus may be hindered. We need to ask the Holy Spirit to begin to unwrap for us any areas in which we are bound.

MANIPULATION, CONTROL AND FEAR OF MAN

by Joyce Meyer

"Am I a God-pleaser, a man-pleaser or a self-pleaser?" I think that is a question we have to ask ourselves regularly. It's easy to start living for self, and it sure is easy to start being a man-pleaser because we all want acceptance and approval. Nobody enjoys rejection.

One way people can easily control others is with the fear and threat of rejection: If you don't keep people happy, you'll be lonely, and you won't have a very good reputation. If you are going to do anything really significant for God, you will have some lonely times. But when there's no one else to turn to but God, you begin to develop a depth you wouldn't have otherwise.

People who are man-pleasers easily come under someone else's manipulation and control, and it makes them mad. But when I complained to the Lord one time about someone trying to control me, He said, "You are just as guilty as they are because you are letting them do it."

God doesn't just see what we do, He sees why we do it. It is easy to get caught up in doing things to serve people. I can pray the most eloquent, powerful sounding prayer, but if I am trying to serve anyone besides God, He won't be pleased. We've got to take off the masks and forget about our reputation. We've got to serve God with a whole heart and do it with right motives, not to get a reputation or to keep everybody on our side.

Paul was going to be brought before Caesar, and he knew that he might be killed (Acts 27:24). But he didn't have his eyes on people, nor on himself. If serving God would cost him his life, he was willing to pay that price. We are never going to do what God called us to if we worry about what everybody thinks.

It's miserable knowing that you kept the people happy, but grieved the Holy Ghost. There's nothing worse than being a slave to other people's expectations. You can kill yourself trying to keep people happy. But if you keep God happy, then He'll keep the people happy—at least the ones who are ever going to be happy. "Whatever may be your task, work at it heartily (from the soul), as [something done] for the Lord and not for men, knowing (with all certainty) that it is from the Lord [and not from men] that you will receive the inheritance which is your (real) reward. [The One Whom] you are actually serving [is] the Lord Christ, the Messiah" (Col. 3:23, 24).

In a manipulative, controlling relationship, the more you try to keep a person happy, the more he demands of you. I used to be really hard to get along with. I was one unhappy, frustrated woman. I was miserable, and I was making everybody around me miserable. My husband, Dave, however, is an easy-going, peace-loving man. For several years, he tried to keep me happy. But one day he looked at me and said, "You know what I've decided? No matter what I do, I'm never going to keep you happy. So I am finished trying. Now you just get it worked out with God."

By trying to keep somebody happy, you can actually block God's working in their life. I'm not saying you should never do what somebody wants you to; I'm not talking about rebellion. And that doesn't mean you shouldn't be nice, kind and loving. Do what you can to get along with people. But there's a line you can cross in trying to please others where you end up grieved and without peace. It feels like you are being pulled in two, because you know it's not what God wants.

Some people are so insecure that when God calls them to do something, if they can't get everyone else on their bandwagon, then they feel unsure about doing it. At that point, they quit serving God and start serving people. Then comes confusion and misery, and God's not going to anoint that mess. Aren't you tired of living your life by what somebody is going to think?

Sometimes people are putting unfair expectations on you. But sometimes you can cook up ideas in your own head about what they're expecting. I don't want to make people mad; but if they get mad, that's not my problem. Love includes freedom to say no.

Let's talk about being a controller. I was manipulated and controlled by my abusive father, forced to do a lot of things and made to act like I liked it. Many times you do things you hate, but you feel compelled to keep a relationship intact or to keep from being talked about or judged. You put on a phoney face and act like it's all wonderful, but inside you despise it.

It is more important what goes on in you than what goes on around you. There will be times when you make a decision where you will have to stand alone, but you've got to do it to have peace with God. Sometimes that involves letting go of some "friendships" you've manipulated into existence.

I once worked hard in a denominational church. I was so insecure. I wanted to be in leadership, and I wanted my husband to be an elder. To be "in the know," I had to be in the "in group." I don't think Dave has ever spent two days in his whole life trying to impress anybody—and everybody just thinks he's wonderful. I about worked myself to death trying to be in the right group, and all I got was rejection. I was being a phoney. Some of the people I was trying to get next to I didn't even like; but I considered them stepping stones to where I wanted to be.

Finally, I got acceptance. But when I was filled with the Holy Spirit, those people I had worked so hard to make friends with, told me they couldn't have any-

thing else to do with me. I remember the pain of that rejection. But I had made a decision that day: God was touching my life, and even if I lost every friend I had, I couldn't go back.

Satan uses the fear of rejection, which is really the fear of man, to keep believers from fulfilling the call of God on their lives. Control is a form of witchcraft. Witches seek to control—to make their influence irresistible.

Paul said, "Now, am I trying to win the favor of men, or of God? Do I seek to be a man-pleaser? If I were still seeking popularity with men, I should not be a bondservant of Christ, the Messiah" (Gal. 1:10). If I were still trying to keep all the people happy, I wouldn't be in ministry.

I distinctly remember when God was promoting me to go the next level of what He had for me. After serving Him faithfully, He said, "Now, I want you to take this ministry and go north, east, south and west." At that time, I was on one radio station. I was well respected, well liked, and had plenty to do. I taught in a Bible college and had a women's meeting every week. I had my own parking place with my name on it, my own seat on the front row, my own office with my name on the door. I didn't have to believe God for my paycheck or everybody else's.

Around that same time, I started getting rejection from everywhere. Everybody I loved was finding something wrong with me, and I had pain and confusion for three years because of it. I was having a hard time even deciding if I was hearing from God or not. I now realize that Satan was launching an attack. It's natural to try to resist the pain of rejection. But that silent message is always there: "If you don't do what I want you to, then you are out."

Take a stand, but don't beat everyone over the head with your Bible. Don't start preaching the minute you walk in the door. That's obnoxious. Wait for the right opportunity. I don't want your friendship if you don't like me for who I am. If I've got to be controlled and manipulated to keep your friendship, I don't want that burden. Neither do I want the burden of trying to control everybody else.

For so many years I thought I was the great choir director of life. Everybody had to do everything my way or not at all. If you are trying to control every circumstance and every person in your life, GIVE IT UP. The pressure and strain of it will kill you. Everybody will end up hating you. Nobody wants to be controlled. Everybody wants space.

Do you have any idea what it was like when Jesus showed up on the scene in that Jewish community? Everything that He taught was diametrically opposed to their regulations. He taught them a whole new way of living. They were always trying to follow the rules, and He was trying to get them to follow the Spirit. "Many even of the leading men—of the authorities *and* the nobles—believed *and* trusted in Him. But because of the Pharisees they did not confess it, for fear [that if they should acknowledge Him] they would be expelled from the synagogue. For they loved the approval *and* the praise *and* the glory that come from men [instead of and] more than the glory that comes from God…They valued their credit with men more than their credit with God" (Jn. 12:42, 43). God was trying to move in their lives. They wanted it, and in their hearts they knew it was right, but the devil said, "You'll be put out of the church." I got put out of my church, but I didn't get put out of the Kingdom.

Some of you are not happy way down deep inside because you are not following the leading of the Holy Ghost for your life. You don't want the pain of loneliness. You don't want to lose what you have now, even though the very things you are trying desperately to hang onto are the things that are making you unhappy. Some of you are wanting something new so bad you can hardly stand it. Yet you are afraid to obey God and let go. God wants you to be free.

Sometimes you find yourself in a position where you know what you want to do. Then all of a sudden, you are talked out of it, and you are doing what everybody else wanted—and you don't even know how it happened! That is manipulation. That means somebody shrewdly and deviously worked the circumstances around to where they are now getting you to do what they want you to do.

Don't be controlled or manipulated. Control and manipulation are wrong, whether you're the perpetrator or the victim. Give people freedom. The Bible says, "Stand fast then, and do not be hampered *and* held ensnared *and* submit again to a yoke of slavery—which you have once put off" (Gal. 5:1).

All Scripture is taken from the Amplified Bible unless otherwise noted.

— Joyce Meyer is the founder of Life in the Word ministry in Fenton, Missouri. She is the author of several books and more than 200 stations worldwide carry her Life in the Word radio program and Life in the Word With Joyce Meyer TV show. She often talks about the abuse she suffered as a child and her failed first marriage. She uses her personal setbacks as real life examples of the power of God in overcoming hardship.

Reprinted by permission: Christ for the Nations. CFNI, P.O. Box 769000, Dallas, TX 75376-9000, 800-933-2364

LESSON 3

UNTIE THE COLT—THE LORD HAS NEED OF IT!

MAIN PRINCIPLE

*God has chosen to use people to fulfill
His plans and purposes on earth.
The Lord wants us loosed from anything holding us in
bondage so that we can be free to do what He needs us to do.*

THE GLORY OF THE UPPER ROOM

by Claudio Freidzon

THE APOSTLE PETER WENT THROUGH THREE YEARS OF STUMBLING, DEFEAT AND INSECURITY—EVEN WHILE HE WALKED WITH CHRIST AND WITNESSED HIS MIRACLES. BUT HE WAS CHANGED FOREVER WHEN THE HOLY SPIRIT TOUCHED HIM.

Signs of a universal spiritual awakening are all around us. We can be excited about that, and we can desire it for the church and for the world. But the fact is, awakening must begin with you and me.

It doesn't happen instantaneously; it is a process. A relationship with God must be developed.

The book of Acts is filled with the experiences of a handful of men who were completely transformed by the Holy Spirit. Peter is one of them. When Jesus called him to be a disciple, He said: " 'You are Simon son of John. You will be called Cephas' (which, when translated, is Peter)" (John 1:42, NIV).

Simon, a temperamental, impulsive fisherman, was given the new name Peter, which means "rock." At the time that Peter was called by the Lord, as well as during his first few years in the ministry, he seemed more like a pebble than a rock. His changeable temperament and his unstable faith had very little in common with the firmness and permanence of a rock.

Yet with eyes of faith, Jesus proclaimed, " 'I also say to you that you are Peter, and on this rock I will build My church' " (Matt. 16:18, NKJV). By calling him a rock, Jesus linked him with solidness and strength.

How marvelous that the Lord should see him this way! He called "things that are not as though they were" (Rom. 4:17, NIV).

How does this kind of transformation come about in our lives? How can we, like Peter, become a rock?

A Rock Relationship

We are speaking of a process—one in which every believer must develop a personal relationship with God. I do not believe in instantaneous transformations; men and women of God are transformed neither by violent nor by abrupt change. A process of transformation is achieved through relationship.

We see this process illustrated in Jesus' parables concerning the development of the kingdom.

In the parable of the sower it is quite evident that God's revelation is progressive (see Matt. 13:1-23). The seed— the Word of God— must fall on good

October 1997, Charisma

soil that has been properly plowed and has been made ready to receive it. Then the seed dies, breaks open and sprouts new life, and finally the fruit appears.

This is never an instantaneous process. Spiritual growth does not develop with the swiftness of modern life and its instant coffee, fast food and high-speed highways. In God's kingdom we are not born as adults but as babies, and we grow under the care of our heavenly Father (see Eph. 4:14-16; 1 Cor. 3:1; Heb. 5:13-14).

This process is also illustrated in the figure of the clay in the potter's hands (see Jer. 18:1-6). Just as the potter shapes the clay, God works progressively through the Holy Spirit to shape us according to the model of His Son, Jesus.

We are not cheap trinkets, imitations of real jewels, which do not take long to produce. We are diamonds that are produced through a long process of being under pressure.

In my own case the process was slow. Some people may think that after attending a worship service or having a pastor lay hands on them, their lives will change instantly. This could be true for some. No doubt God can use other ministries to complete the work that He has been doing in our hearts.

But it was not so for me. I had to go through long times of divine dealing, waiting, preparation and brokenheartedness to be molded for the stage in which I live today.

Whatever stage we may be going through in our Christian walk, there is a difference between being filled with the Holy Spirit and not being filled.

Peter went through a period of stumbling, defeat and insecurity. But Jesus had promised the disciples they would receive power when the Holy Spirit came on them. His promise became a reality for Peter in the upper room as he and the rest of the people gathered there were filled with the Holy Spirit. The experience recorded in Acts 2 marked Peter's life from that moment on.

Peter walked with Jesus for three years. He lived through the most glorious moments of the Lord's ministry. He witnessed how Jesus healed the blind and calmed the sea.

When he had to make a stand for Christ, however, he refused to do so. But after he received the fulfillment of Christ's promise in the upper room, the fullness of the Holy Spirit enabled him to become a faithful witness.

The lesson is clear. We do not change because we witness miracles and wonders, nor do we change because we attend a beautiful worship service. Only an upper-room experience can transform us—a personal experience with Christ through His Holy Spirit.

Accustomed to God

In Argentina in the 1980's, the Lord raised up a famous and formidable evangelist named Carlos Annacondia. Through his ministry the Lord performed miracles that were an accompaniment to the preaching of the word.

But in time it became evident that there was great danger ahead. Many of the believers who had witnessed supernatural manifestations in the life and ministry of Annacondia reacted in a different way in the 1990s. They seemed to lose interest in the things of God.

Carlos told me that many of those who at one time supported his crusades were no longer doing so. Why? Because they had become *accustomed* to the supernatural. Remember: A change of heart does not occur simply as a result of witnessing miracles and wonders.

Change did not occur in the case of the soldiers who went to arrest Jesus. When they found the Lord, they fell to the ground as He acknowledged His identity (see Mark 14:48-49). But then they got up—and crucified Him.

Change did not occur in the case of Israel either. Only three months after leaving Egypt and seeing so many miracles and wonders performed in their midst, they left God to commit the terrible sin of idolatry. How

October 1997, Charisma

could they do it? I believe there are three answers:

They had become accustomed to the supernatural, to the glory of God.
In Exodus 19 the people evidenced fear in the presence of the glory of God on Mount Sinai. They were moved.

But then they began to get accustomed to the glory and became indifferent to it. Perhaps they said, "This is something we see every day!" Even before Moses descended from the mountain, they had forsaken their faith.

They took the Word of God lightly.

This is what God told them: " 'You shall have no other gods before Me. You shall not make for yourself a carved image—any likeness of anything that is in heaven above, or that is in the earth beneath, or that is in the water under the earth' " (Ex. 20:3-4, NKJV). But they sinned because they did not take God's Word seriously.

They did not cultivate a personal relationship with God.

The Israelites failed to express their love for God in the manner emphasized to them by Moses (see Deut. 6:5; 7:9). They said to Moses, " 'You speak to God and tell Him…and ask Him.' " They did not attempt to establish a personal relationship with God on their own; they relied on a middleman.

Let us refuse to live on borrowed faith! It is our relationship with God that counts in the final analysis. Only in an intimate walk with Him will we experience marvelous changes.

The fact is, there are two things that nobody else can do for us: Have faith, and hunger for God. These things lead to the experience of a victorious life. Let's look at them more closely:

1. No one can have faith for you.

To have faith is to obey God. It is to be filled with His faith, to believe His Word, to believe everything He promises us.

The people of Israel kept forgetting the precious promises given to them by God. In Psalm 105 we read about the glorious wonders that God had done among them, but Psalm 106 reveals the attitude the people adopted: "They forgot the God who saved them, who had done great things in Egypt, miracles in the land of Ham and awesome deeds by the Red Sea" (Ps. 106:21-22, NIV). The book of Hebrews says they lost the land "because of their unbelief" (Heb. 3:19).

Faith is a characteristic sign of every man and woman of God. "Without faith it is impossible to please God" (Heb. 11:6). We received eternal life when we expressed faith in the righteousness He obtained for us on the cross at Calvary. That is how our Christian lives began, and that is how we should continue.

When I had my personal encounter with the Lord, I opened my heart to Him and said, "Lord, if You really love me and care for me, come into my heart." And He came into my life!

From the first instant, I saw the world in a different light. I looked at nature and at people with different eyes.

I had been born again, and that new birth urged me forward to achieve new goals, take new steps and go on to new stages. In that wonderful life of faith, the Lord called me to ascend mountains I never imagined in order to be with Him.

2. No one can hunger for God in your place.

To hunger for God is to long to be filled by God. Jesus said, "Blessed are those who hunger and thirst for righteousness" (Matt. 5:6).

These words imply that we are to hunger for Christ and thirst for a life lived the way He lived His. We want the reality of the kingdom of God to be seen in our manner of living, in the way we bring up our children and in the way we conduct ourselves in society. Our lives become faith made visible.

October 1997, Charisma

A hunger and longing for the glory of God in greater measure caused me to seek His face with all my heart. As a result, in 1992, I experienced a powerful flow of the one who was within me.

Many people believe that God works in their lives from the outside in, but Jesus clearly taught that streams of living water would flow "from within" us (John 7:38). The Word teaches us that " ' the one who is in you is greater than the one who is in the world' " (1 John 4:4).

There is a fountain within us, a life that is locked up, a river that is held in. For it to flow, we need to be broken, humbled and wholly dependent on the Lord.

Imagine for a moment that you approach the ocean nearest your home and pick up a small amount of sea water in a little cup. The difference between what you have in your cup and what you see before you is like the difference between what you know of God and what He really is—a mere drop in an immense sea.

In these times God calls us to feel unsatisfied, to cry out: "Lord, I need you. I'm not satisfied with what I have. I want more of You and more of Your presence. I'm not yet satisfied because I know I've received only a small portion of that great ocean."

Let us use our hunger for God, coupled with our faith in God, as the catalysts that birth revival in our hearts.

Toward a Great Awakening

During the last few years of intense ministry I have observed many impressive manifestations of the Holy Spirit. But recently God revealed His will for the church in these times.

As Jeremiah instructed, " 'This is what the Lord says: Stand at the crossroads and look; ask for the ancient paths, ask where the good way is, and walk in it, and you will find rest for your souls' " (Jer. 6:16). The church must get back to the ancient paths. We must go back to the basic principles of the Word.

The New Testament opens with the commandments of the Lord Jesus, which upheld the awakening experienced by the New Testament church and will be the foundation of His work in us today. The ancient paths lead to the preaching of the need for genuine and honest repentance, which every Christian must express to God.

We have witnessed the Holy Spirit wondrously bless the church with His power. We have seen people falling under the power of God and remaining prostrate before Him for hours; entire stadiums of people enjoying His presence; and people dancing in His presence.

But beyond these manifestations must come real encounters with God that produce repentance and confession of sins. Jesus called men to repentance and then to obedience, the fruit of repentance.

The first evidence of obedience is baptism in water. Then comes the baptism in the Holy Spirit that John the Baptist anticipated: " 'After me will come one who…will baptize you with the Holy Spirit and with fire' " (Matt. 3:11). The word *fire* is symbolic of the Holy Spirit. Fire purifies, consumes and transforms.

Under the power of the Holy Spirit we may fall, tremble or laugh, but none of these manifestations will change us, and we must not set our eyes on them. What will *change* our lives is the fire that fell on Pentecost, the same fire that was evident in the lives of the apostles. That's what brings spiritual awakening. And it must begin with each of us.

Adapted from *Holy Spirit, I Hunger for You* by Claudio Freidzon, copyright 1997. Published by Creation House. Used by permission.

—Claudio Freidzon was born near Buenos Aires, Argentina in 1955. In 1986 he founded the King of Kings Church in Argentina. Claudio Freidzon is also the best selling author of *Holy Spirit, I Hunger For You!* and *From Glory To Glory*.

Reprinted by permission *Charisma Magazine* and Strang Communications Company.

October 1997, Charisma

LESSON 4

JESUS, OUR PASSOVER LAMB

MAIN PRINCIPLE

We can come to God only because of the atoning work of Christ, our Passover Lamb. As His blood covers us by faith, we can abide in God's glory.

THE LAMB OF GOD

<u>PASSOVER</u>	<u>JESUS</u>
On the 10th day of Nisan, a male lamb was selected.	Jesus entered Jerusalem on the 10th day of Nisan.
Lambs were observed for spot or blemish for five days.	Jesus was tested for five days by Jewish and Roman leaders.
Priests of Jesus' day prepared lambs for sacrifice at 9 AM.	Jesus was crucified at 9 AM.
Blood of the lambs was painted on doorways.	The Lamb of God shed His blood.
Lambs were roasted on a spit shaped like a crossbar.	Jesus was nailed on a cross.
Priests of Jesus' day sacrificed the lambs at 3 PM.	Jesus died at 3 PM.
None of the lamb was to be left until the next day.	Jesus was removed from the cross before the Sabbath.
Only people in houses covered by blood were saved from death.	Only people accepting Jesus' blood sacrifice are saved from sin and death.
Only people in a blood covenant with the Hebrew God could celebrate the Passover.	Only people in a blood covenant with God through Jesus can come into His presence.

From pages 18–28 of Richard Booker's *Jesus in the Feasts of Israel,*
Bridge Publishing, Inc., South Plainfield, New Jersey, 1987.
Used by permission from author.

ASSIGNED ARTICLE

GOD SO LOVED THE WORLD

by Judson Cornwall

HE GAVE US HIS SON. AND THROUGH THE EYES OF THE APOSTLE JOHN
WE CAN SEE THE INTENSITY AND DEPTH OF THAT LOVE.

I have often been intrigued by how differently people view the same set of circumstances. Some years ago, when I was serving on a jury, I was struck by the contrasting and often conflicting testimonies of the witnesses. There was no reason to believe anyone was lying; each person simply saw the incident from a different perspective and filtered it through his or her particular mind-set.

It was much the same way with Jesus' disciples. Each saw the same miracles and heard the same teachings, but those who wrote down their accounts assessed the circumstances differently. For instance, Peter saw the God-man, while John saw the nature of God in the man. Perhaps these viewpoints are rooted in the different natures of these men. Peter, the fisherman, was a "people person" whom Jesus called to be a "fisher of men," while John was described as the great apostle of love. He was the mystic, the man of foresight to whom the vision of the book of Revelation was given.

In his writings, John modestly refrained from referring to himself directly, but he was the disciple who stayed with Jesus throughout the Lord's arrest, trial and crucifixion. He saw the thorny crown being pressed into Christ's head, and for years he would hear the swish of the Roman cat-o'-nine-tails as Jesus was scourged at the whipping post.

It is likely that John was but a few steps behind Jesus as He wound His way along the Via Dolorosa to the Golgotha. John stood with the mother of Jesus as the Roman spikes were driven through the wrists and ankles of Jesus. He watched in horror as the cross was raised skyward and then dropped into a hole in the earth with such force as to dislodge the arms from their sockets.

John listened to the mocking crowd and the jeers of the soldiers. He marveled as Jesus responded on the cross by praying, "Father, forgive them, for they do not know what they do" (Luke 23:34, NKJV). John saw the love of Jesus extended to a thief hanging on a cross by His side. Finally, in a triumphant exclamation of love, Jesus cried to the Father, "It is finished!" (John 19:30), and died. Jesus had demonstrated His love by giving His life!

No wonder John's account of the life of Jesus is so often called the Gospel of love. Matthew and Luke begin their Gospels with the genealogy of Christ through the lineage of His earthly parents. But John begins his Gospel by giving the *divine* lineage of Jesus. He wrote, "In the beginning was the Word, and the Word was with God, and the Word was God. He was in the beginning with God…And the Word became flesh and dwelt among us…" (John 1:1, 2, 14).

Matthew and Luke were concerned with the events surrounding Jesus' birth, but John's mind turned to the reason Christ was born. He made the powerful declaration that "God so loved the world that He gave His only begotten Son, that whoever believes in Him should not perish but have everlasting life" (John 3:16). John did not see humanity's condition as the motivating force behind the divine incarnation; he saw God's divine love as the impelling power of the incarnation.

Love is demonstrable—how else would we know it is? A popular syndicated cartoon is titled simply "Love is…" and the cartoonist gives us a daily picture of love, reinforcing that it is a lifestyle, an attitude expressed or a reaction to an action. Love is unselfish, costly giving that benefits the recipient more than the giver, for "God demonstrates His own love toward us, in that while we were still sinners, Christ died for us" (Rom. 5:8).

Calvary is the supreme demonstration of divine love. Is there a person alive today who can fathom the depths of such love? Can our most learned theologians give us any rational reason for a sinless, holy, eternal, immutable, glorious, moral, almighty God to love such debased, wretched, immoral, rebellious, condemned and hell-bent sinners such as we? Our finite minds cannot grasp the infinite love of an eternal God, but our faith can appropriate it to the changing of our lives. John summarized our proof of God's love for us in these simple words: "By this we know love, because He laid down His life for us" (1 John 3:16).

That God would forgive our sins would be wonder enough, but that He would actually take our place as a substitute on the cross is a wonder of wonders. That will take all of eternity to unravel the mystery. For the present we must accept the limited statement of the scripture that "God so loved…."

In his first epistle John wrote, "God is love. In this the love of God was manifested toward us, that God has sent His only begotten Son into the world, that we might live through Him" (1 John 4:8, 9).

John's declaration that "God is love" defines God's essential nature in the highest conception we humans can hold. It forces us to believe that the divine love is eternal and unchangeable—it is "that which was from the beginning" (1 John 1:1)—and it requires us to believe that His love governs all other attributes in the Godhead, for to say "God is love" implies that all His activity is loving activity. God rules in love; He chastens in love; He relates to us in love. Furthermore, this revelation makes us aware that God's love to humanity originated entirely with Himself, and that God is the fountain of all love. "Love is of God…God is love," John wrote (1 John 4:7, 8).

The apostle continued, "In this is love, not that we loved God, but that He loved us and sent His Son to be the propitiation for our sins" (1 John 4:10). The incarnation and atonement constitute the revelation of God's love. John's contemporaries saw the persons who were involved in the incarnation and the trappings that surrounded it, but John saw the love of God manifested in that event. While other values in life can imitate God's love, only Jesus actually and fully communicates that love.

Christ's mission was to reveal God's love, and John caught sight of this. While the synoptic Gospels repeatedly report the things Jesus did, John wrote of the things Jesus said. He wrote of only seven miracles that Jesus performed, and then he generally used them as audio-visuals to set the stage for Jesus' teaching. John stood less in awe of Christ's miracles than of the revelation of who He was.

—Judson Cornwall was a prolific charismatic Christian preacher, pastor and author of over 50 books on varied subjects such as worship, praise, spiritual warfare and death. He began preaching at age 7 and later was regarded as an apostle, who ministered worldwide. Cornwall passed away in 2005. Three of his books, *Let Us Worship*, *Elements of Worship*, and *Let Us Praise*, are widely considered Christian classics.

Excerpted from *Meeting God*, by Judson Cornwall, copyright 1987. Published by Creation House, Altamonte Springs, Florida. Used by permission

WHY THE CROSS?

by Ray Vander Laan

DURING THE TIME OF CHRIST, CRUCIFIXION WAS A REGULAR OCCURRENCE. SO WHAT MADE JESUS' CRUCIFIXION ANY DIFFERENT?

I've conducted hundreds of tours to Israel, and the same thing happens each time I lead the group to the Garden Tomb in Jerusalem. Located just outside the city, it is one of the suggested sites for Golgotha. One of the first questions I'm asked is, "Why was Jesus crucified here?"

"Archeological evidence seems to indicate He wasn't," I reply as we stand at the base of a rocky cliff. "I also believe that Jesus was not crucified on the top of a hill, but at the foot, similar to where we are now standing."

"The Romans introduced crucifixion to Israel," I continue. "Jews had previously put people guilty of blasphemy and sexual immorality to death by stoning, but the Romans crucified their victims at the base of a hill so the condemned would be easily seen by passersby."

During Palestine's 400 year occupation by Rome, thousands were crucified, and this form of execution was governed by specific rules. The idea was to make this horrible procedure as painful as possible—and an example to others. Jesus' long suffering on the Cross was dreadful.

Directed by Almighty God, no events have been more central and history-changing than the Crucifixion and Resurrection of the Messiah. Before crucifixion existed, ancient biblical texts revealed God's carefully detailed plans regarding Jesus' death. Let's take a look at the facts:

Roman Customs

1. Roman crucifixion took place in a public location outside the city (Psalm 22:6-7, 17).
2. The Romans usually crucified people naked (Matthew 27:35).
3. Romans preferred a cross in the shape of an upper-case T rather than a lower-case t. Crosses were quite low, only 5 to 6 feet off the ground (Matthew 27:48).
4. The condemned person was nailed to the cross through the wrists and ankles. In John 20:27, the Greek word for "hand" refers to the part of the arm from the palm to the wrist. Evidence indicates that the spikes were driven through the bones of the arm where they join at the wrist.

Roman Procedures

1. The Romans first flogged the condemned person, which often left the prisoner near death (John 19:1; Isaiah 53:5).
2. The cross bar was tied to the prisoner's shoulders. He was paraded through the streets for humiliation and as an example (Psalm 22:6). A soldier carried a sign indicating the crime the person had

committed (John 19:16-19).

3. At the place of execution, the prisoner's wrists were nailed to the crossbar. The bar was lifted and placed on the stake, which was already in the ground. The condemned person's ankles were then nailed to the stake. The prisoner, in excruciating pain, eventually died of asphyxiation and loss of blood (Psalm 22:14,16; John 19:19).

4. Prisoners could remain conscious for days. Sometimes the Roman soldiers shortened the prisoner's suffering by breaking his legs. Because his legs no longer supported the weight of his body, he suffocated faster. Jesus died without any broken bones (John 19:33; Exodus 12:46; Exodus 34:20).

5. Roman soldiers kept the victim's possessions (Matthew 27:35; Psalm 22:18).

6. Prisoners could talk only in short bursts because of the stress on their diaphragms. As Jesus hung on the cross, His statements were short:

- "Father, forgive them, for they do not know what they are doing" (Luke 23:34).
- "I tell you the truth, today you will be with me in paradise" (Luke 23:43).
- "My God, my God, why have you forsaken me?" (Matthew 27:46; Psalm 22:1).
- "I am thirsty" (John 19:28).
- "It is finished" (John 19:30).
- "Father, into your hands I commit my spirit" (Luke 23:46).

The Lamb of God

During my Israel tours I explain to the group that Jesus had arrived in Jerusalem on the 10th day of the Jewish month—the day the Passover lamb was chosen for the Passover offering. As each Jewish family selected a lamb to die on Passover (Exodus 12:3), their most passionate desire was for a Messiah, a savior, to come. Jesus' arrival on this particular day was as if God was saying, "Here's my lamb. Will you choose Him?"

Could the similarity between the Passover lamb and Jesus' destiny to become God's sacrificial Lamb for the sins of the world be *just* a coincidence? Traditionally, the daily sacrifice was slaughtered at 3 o'clock in the afternoon, including on the day of Passover. At that time, the priest stood at the pinnacle of the temple and blew the *shofar*, or ram's horn.

As Jesus hung on the Cross, He heard the piercing blast of the *shofar* carry across the city. Jesus recognized that the hour of His sacrifice had come. When the knife slit the throat of the Passover lamb, Jesus looked up to heaven and said, "It is finished." At that moment, the Passover lamb and God's substitute—our Passover Lamb—died at 3 p.m.

Jesus is the Lamb of God who takes away your sins and the sins of the world. Have you asked God's Son to forgive you for your wrong actions and attitudes? Is salvation your greatest need? If so, you can accept Jesus for who He really is and receive eternal life.

A "Politically Correct" Messiah

Culturally, Passover was a time when the Jewish longing for a messiah intensified. Jewish tradition states that the Temple door was to remain open on Passover eve—just in case the Messiah arrived.

During this festival Jewish people celebrated deliverance from Egyptian bondage but in Jesus' time it angered them that Jerusalem was under foreign control. Messianic fervor fueled a dangerous atmosphere.

Antonia, the Roman fortress that housed Roman soldiers in Jerusalem was located at the north end of the Temple Mount. During Passover, Antonia was reinforced with extra troops. Episodes involving bloodshed during Passover were not unusual.

Nationalistic Jews used the people's awareness of prophecy to declare themselves as messiahs to gain a following which sometimes erupted into riots. Messiahs and their followers who created problems for the Romans were often killed. Making a public spectacle was tantamount to a death wish.

Why would the Romans feel threatened by a Jewish rabbi from Galilee riding a donkey and surrounded by a joyful crowd waving palm branches?

When Jesus entered Jerusalem the people chanted, "Hosanna" and shouted, "Please save us, O son of David!" (Matthew 21:9). In effect, they were proclaiming Jesus as a military and political savior. The Jews wanted a warrior-messiah who, like David, triumphed over the enemy.

Hosanna, a nationalistic chant, had become a prayer for political deliverance. It meant "Give me my freedom." Originally, hosanna and the palms were linked to the Jewish feast of Sukkot, which included the hosanna prayer from Psalm 118:25-26. Composed of two Hebrew words *hosha* meant "save" and *na* added a sense of urgency. Thus, hosanna meant "Please save," or "Help, please!"

The palm, a symbol of Jewish national identity, had little to do with peace and love. Palm branches were to the Jews what the Stars and Stripes are to Americans. The waving of the palm branches led Jesus to weep.

When messianic anticipation was at its highest, Jesus proclaimed His messianic identity. Those assembled along the road into Jerusalem did not recognize Jesus' true identity as the promised Messiah who would bring *eternal* salvation (Zechariah 9:9-10), not just destroy the enemy of the day.

— Ray Vander Laan founded That the World May Know Ministries in 1998. An ordained minister in the Christian Reformed Church, he has taken over 10,000 people with him on his study tours of Israel, Turkey and Egypt. Vander Laan's preaching and teaching ministry is focused on understanding the Bible in light of the historical and cultural context in which God placed it.

Focus on the Family magazine, March 1977

THE POWER OF JESUS' BLOOD

by Derek Kuhn

In Romans 3:25, Paul says, "…God set forth (Jesus) as a propitiation by His blood, through faith…." Scripture encourages us to place our faith in the blood of Jesus. Andrew Murray in his commentary on the book of Hebrews says, "Our faith must be quickened to expect the all-conquering power of the blood."

But we cannot truly exercise faith unless we know what the Bible says about the Blood of Jesus. "…Faith comes by hearing, and hearing by the word of God" (Rom. 10:17). As we hear about the blood of Christ and what the blood of His cross has accomplished, our hearing will give way to faith in our hearts.

After we have heard the Word of truth about the blood, we must put our trust in it. We hear with our ears, and with our minds we perceive and understand, but "…with the heart one believes…" (Rom. 10:10). Something must happen in our hearts to convince us to place our trust, hope and confidence in the blood.

Faith needs to be released through verbal declaration. "…With the mouth confession is made unto salvation" (Rom. 10:10). We must declare what the blood has accomplished—at the Cross, in our lives and through us. We tap into the power of the blood by declaring what the scripture has to say about the Blood. "And they overcame him by the blood of the Lamb, and by the word of their testimony, and they did not love their lives to the death" (Rev. 12:11).

The protective power of the blood is demonstrated in Israel's exodus from Egypt. "And the blood shall be a sign for you on the houses where you are. And when I see the blood, I will pass over you; and the plague shall not be on you to destroy you, when I strike the land of Egypt" (Ex. 12:13). God did not choose to spare the Israelites because of their nationality or lineage from Abraham; the blood was the only reason they did not die. Not only did blood have to be shed, but it had to be applied to the doorposts of their homes. Today, the application of the blood takes place through our faith. The infinite power of Christ's blood becomes effective in our lives and ministers to our own needs, and through us—to the needs of others.

If you remove the blood of Jesus from Christianity, you remove the power of the atonement. The Bible says without the shedding of blood, there is no forgiveness (Heb. 9:22). The law of blood sacrifice states in Leviticus 17:11, "For the life of the flesh is in the blood; and I have given it to you upon the altar to make atonement for your souls; for it is the blood that makes atonement for the soul."

Jesus lived a life of complete obedience, "…a lamb without blemish and without spot" (I Pet. 1:19). His obedience brought about the righteousness of which we would become partakers by faith. He suffered and laid down his life so God would forgive our sins. God didn't say He would forgive everybody. He cannot overlook sin or be indifferent to it. His forgiveness is based on the atonement of Jesus Christ and the blood that was shed upon the cross.

It cost Jesus His life to bring about the forgiveness that we today enjoy. In the Garden of Gethsemane, Jesus said, "…O my Father, *if it is possible,* let this cup pass from Me; nevertheless, not as I will, but as You will"

(Matt. 26:39). God would have answered Jesus' plea in the Garden if there had been another way to forgive people on earth. But there was no other way. The Father in heaven was not indifferent to the suffering of His Son. But He loved us so much that He gave His Son, and the Son loved us so much that He was willing to do the will of God (Jn. 3:16). That is the new righteousness that totally crushed Satan's head. Romans 5:18 says, "Therefore, as through one man's offense judgment came to all men, resulting in condemnation, even so through one Man's righteous act the free gift came to all men, resulting in justification of life."

The devil can never imprison righteousness; that's why death could not hold Jesus in the grave. Neither can the devil exercise authority and dominion over obedience. The most excruciating pain that a man could experience physically, Jesus endured for us. No man ever experienced what Jesus experienced when He became sin.

As we begin to grasp what the Bible has to say about crucifixion and resurrection, it will become a source of power and authority in our lives. The devil can never, never overcome the blood of the Lamb. Rather, we overcome him by the blood of the Lamb. The devil can never overcome those areas in your life that are under the blood. He can only take dominion over those areas that are not.

So put every area of your life under the blood. God has not effected a partial salvation or half victories. Every home in Egypt that applied the blood to the doorpost was safe.

Jesus' whole life was lived through the power of the Spirit. He was conceived by the Holy Spirit. He was baptized with the Holy Spirit. He performed miracles by the power of the Spirit. He was even led into the wilderness by the Spirit. Whatever God does in redemption, He does by the power of His Spirit.

There is resurrection power in the blood. "Now may the God of peace who brought up our Lord Jesus from the dead, that great Shepherd of the sheep, through the blood of the everlasting covenant…" (Heb.13:20). Christ rose triumphantly by the blood of the everlasting covenant.

When we come into a situation with death written all over it, we need to begin to declare and speak the Blood of the everlasting covenant into that situation. Suddenly, that satanic grip will lose its power. Satan has to let go of that which is under the blood! When you start speaking about the blood, immediately the Holy Spirit comes on the scene. The blood attracts the Holy Spirit; through faith, we begin to discover the power of the blood of Jesus.

—Adapted from a message given by Derek Kuhn at CFNI and from his study outline and notes entitled "Discover the Power of the Blood of Jesus."

Derek Kuhn is a traveling pastor, teacher and apostolic prophetic singer. Dr. Kuhn is currently the pastor at Grace Covenant Worship Center in Highland Park, Illinois.

Reprinted by permission: Christ for the Nations. CFNI, P.O. Box 769000, Dallas, TX 75376-9000, 800-933-2364

LESSON 5

BETRAYAL VERSUS LOVE

MAIN PRINCIPLE

God wants us to extend extravagant love toward Jesus. Are we willing to give to Jesus anything He asks us of us because He laid down His life for us? Are we willing to lay down our own plans and ambitions for Him? Are we willing to show our love for Jesus despite what people will think?

ASSIGNED ARTICLE

THE TRUTH ABOUT JUDAS— BETRAYER OF CHRIST

by David Wilkerson

"JUDAS ISCARIOT, WHICH ALSO WAS THE BETRAYER" (LUKE 6:16).

He was a handpicked disciple of Jesus Christ: a preacher of the gospel, a healer of the sick, a traveling companion of Jesus. He was so trusted he was made treasurer of the apostolic evangelistic team. He wasn't elected to the position—Jesus personally chose Judas for the job.

According to Augustine, tradition says "Jesus had delivered Judas often from death, and for his sake healed his father of palsy and cured his mother of leprosy, and next to Peter he honored him above all the other apostles."

But we do know certain things about Judas as fact: that Jesus washed his feet, let him dip his bread in His own cup, and made him His treasurer. Yet this was the very man who would betray Jesus in the Garden of Gethsemane—with a kiss of death!

Judas led the wild mob of Jewish officers to the garden, where he identified Christ with a kiss. After the kiss, Jesus looked into Judas' eyes and said, "Judas, betrayest thou the Son of man with a kiss?" (Luke 22:48). He was saying, "Is that how you would betray me, Judas—with a kiss, a sign of affection?"

I wonder what went through Judas' mind as the scene unfolded:

The mob fell backward at the very mention of Jesus' name. Then suddenly they all rose up in demonic anger, waving swords and clubs—and they bound Christ and dragged Him to the house of Annas. Early church writers described the scene this way:

"Some of them lay hold on his garments, others on the hair of his head: some pluck him by the beard, others struck him with angry fists, and being enraged, that with a word he had thrown them backwards on the ground, they therefore threw him on his back, and basely tread him under their dirty feet.... As a roaring lion drags along the earth his prey, and tears it, and pulls it, so they hauled Christ all along the earth, spitting, pounding on him, pulling him by the hair...."

This is confirmed by the Scriptures: "Many bulls have compassed me: strong bulls of Bashan have beset me round. They gaped upon me with their mouths, as a ravening and a roaring lion" (Psalm 22:12-13).

Judas' betrayal of Jesus was so heinous, so diabolical, that one early church father said: "It would have been well for the world, especially for the children of God, that Judas was alone in this transgression, that there were no more traitorous persons in it besides himself." In other words: It would have been good if there had been only one Judas.

But the truth is, the world is full of Judas' kind! The church still witnesses the betrayal of Jesus Christ every day. The spirit of Judas is very much alive in the hearts of many former followers of Christ—and within the walls of the church as well!

I want to ask you a blunt, up-front question: Could you be a traitor to Christ and not know it? Have you sold out Jesus and betrayed Him? Traitors are those who once were loyal to the one they betray. Only those within the camp can be traitors.

There are two facts I want to share with you about Judas. They may surprise you—but please do not take them lightly. I believe they were given to me by the Holy Spirit as a warning for your soul!

Fact Number One: The High Priests and Religious Leaders Did Not Need Judas to Seize Christ.

Jesus could easily have been captured without Judas' help. He had taught in the synagogues, streets and marketplaces. His face was one of the most recognizable in all Israel and Judah. Scripture says the people followed Him even to the quiet places where He withdrew to pray!

Jesus said to the arresting mob, "Are ye come out as against a thief with swords and staves for to take me? I sat daily with you teaching in the temple, and ye laid no hold on me" (Matthew 26:55). In other words: "I am well known to you—My face is familiar. Why this sudden attack as though I were a complete stranger to you?"

Clearly Judas' kiss was not needed to identify Christ—because Christ's enemies knew Him well already! His face was emblazoned on their consciences. And the aura of His mighty presence was itself enough to identify Him.

Indeed, it is clear the perpetrators of this crime did not need Judas. The fact is, they despised him. They treated him lightly, using him and then quickly pushing him aside. When he repented suddenly of his traitorous deed, flinging the money to the ground and crying, "I have betrayed the innocent blood" (Matthew 27:4), the Jewish leaders merely laughed at him.

They said, "What is that to us? See thou to that" (verse 4), meaning, "That's your problem—take care of it yourself. We have no need of you or your tears!"

Judas wasn't needed for Jesus' trial or crucifixion, either. In fact, he wasn't around for either one. By the time Christ went to the Cross, Judas was already dead, having committed suicide within twenty-four hours of his awful deed.

Fact Number Two: Satan Needed a Judas!

Satan was behind the scenes, directing every treacherous move. His strategy was to find a betrayer—someone close to Christ, someone He trusted, one who supposedly was under His care. Yet he had to have one whose heart was tilted to covetousness—someone he could entice and weaken, planting questions and doubts in his mind. Then he could possess him and turn him into a traitor!

You see, Satan wanted much more than to have his demon-directed mob go into the garden and take hold of Jesus. He wanted the whole affair to make a statement—to be a satanic witness! He wanted a demonic testimony to ring loudly in every realm of creation. And here is the statement he wanted to make:

"Jesus Christ cannot keep you—He can't even deliver His own! He is not a true Savior or a Keeper of men's souls. He failed to keep Judas—and He failed to keep me, one of His angels, and all the others who fell with me. I'm going to prove that Jesus has no power to keep anyone from falling. He will give you up to your enemy!"

Judas was to be the devil's illustrated sermon on how Jesus Christ was powerless to save the lost—because He did not save His very own disciple!

Satan wanted it to appear as if he had snatched Judas right out of the Master's hands. He wanted to show he had the power to approach anyone close to Jesus and take him at will—and that Jesus would let it happen! He could march right into the Lord's flock as a roaring lion, steal a lamb in his teeth, and damn and destroy him, causing him to commit suicide.

Finally, when the time would come to push Judas to kill himself, Satan would scream out his testimony to all of hell, heaven and the world: "Do you see what has become of this man? Look at him— he was a disciple of Jesus. But Jesus couldn't keep him!"

Satan had to have a Judas! He wanted to use him to proclaim his demonic statement to three different realms:

1. Satan first wanted to make a statement to all the principalities and powers of darkness. I believe the devil planned to use Judas' fall to justify his own fall and the fall of those angels who joined in his rebellion!

If the devil could destroy a close disciple of Jesus— one who himself had cast out devils, healed the sick, performed miracles and walked in the fullest light of truth—then he could say to every fallen angel and demonic power: "See? God's love is flawed. His compassions do fail! It was prophesied long ago that Judas would come, and yet God did nothing to protect or save him.

"God could have kept me too—He could have kept all of us from pride. But now you can clearly see that God again has failed to keep His own!"

2. Satan also wanted to make a statement to all the holy angels. He sought to throw darts of doubt into heaven itself to corrupt the unfallen, uncorrupted witnesses in glory.

Don't think for a moment the devil has given up his struggle to bring down the heavens and exalt himself as God. He is the accuser of not just the brethren, but of all that is of God—including the angels!

After Judas' suicide, Satan screamed to those in glory: "God couldn't save one of His very own disciples— and He didn't keep us, His created angels. What makes you think He'll keep you?

"He created man, and now it is clear He can't keep man. His own kind betray him! So what hinders another rebellion among you?"

We know the battle still rages, that Satan still fights the heavenly hosts. He fought the archangel Michael, who sought to bring the Word of God to Daniel. And surely today he uses every lie and diabolic strategy to try to plant doubt and rebellion in the hosts of Jehovah!

3. Most of all, Satan's statement was meant for mankind—for you and me! The message he sent was meant primarily for God's people on earth. He wants to use it to destroy all faith!

The devil knows the Scriptures well—and he knew that all following generations would look back upon first occurrences as examples "upon whom the ends of the world are come" (1 Corinthians 10:11). Satan wanted an example too—a pattern to show every following generation what he claimed was God's failure to keep His own children from failing. The betrayal by Judas was meant to shake and undermine the faith of God's children in His saving, keeping power.

So what, the devil says, if Jesus exposed Judas as a "devil": "Have not I chosen you twelve, and one of you is a devil?" (John 6:70). Satan replies, "That's all the more testimony to my power! If Jesus knew Judas had the devil in him, then why didn't He overpower me? Why did He let Judas continue as a devil? Why didn't He cast me out?

"If God couldn't take care of His own disciples, how can He take care of you?"

Beloved, the enemy wants to plant a seed of doubt in the minds of all men and women—and he will repeat his message time after time, as long as the Lord has a church on the earth. He will cry out from generation to generation, right up to eternity: "God cannot keep His children!"

Imagine what the high priests and the Sanhedrin must have thought as they bargained with Judas, the pitiful man before them. They saw this devilish example betraying Christ and falling into ruin. They must have said to themselves, "We're right! Jesus is not God, or the Son of God. If He were, He would have kept this disciple from falling."

You can see them opening their scrolls, quoting: "It is written by the Psalmist, "Behold, he that keepeth Israel shall neither slumber nor sleep. The Lord is thy keeper.... The sun shall not smite thee by day, nor the moon by night. The Lord shall preserve thee from all evil" (Psalm 121:4-7). If Jesus were God, He would have fulfilled this Scripture!

"Also, it is written: "Surely he shall deliver thee from the snare of the fowler... There shall no evil befall thee, neither shall any plague come nigh thy dwelling" (Psalm 91:3, 10). Jesus cannot be God, because He allowed Judas to be snared. Evil befell this man—and he was a close disciple!" You can hear Satan shouting to their inner man: "If Jesus is God, why isn't He keeping this man? Why isn't Judas being delivered?"

A few weeks ago, during our Friday prayer meeting, we heard the testimony of a mother and her teenage daughter who had been attacked by a mob of youth. The mob ripped the girl's clothes and beat her mother. Somehow, they escaped without further harm.

When they came forward to testify, the mother was wearing sunglasses to hide her eyes, blackened from the beating. Now the daughter is struggling with her faith. She said to me tearfully, "Look at my lip—a girl bit me there, and I have the scar for life. Pastor David, my mother has served the Lord for so long. Why did God allow this to happen to us? Why didn't His promises work? Where was He?"

A couple of months ago, fires and lootings spread through Los Angeles. But for the first few days of those riots, all the Teen Challenge centers in that area were spared, including a huge warehouse in the heart of the city. That warehouse is used to store clothes and appliances, which are sold at base prices to help the poor and needy.

Then, on the third or fourth day of the riots, the warehouse was burned to the ground. Some 5,000 square feet of goods and space were completely destroyed. Nothing was left!

Some of the young Teen Challenge converts questioned: "Where was the angel of the Lord? Where was the protection? This was a good work in God's name. Why did He allow it to be destroyed?"

In These Troubled Times, When All Is Being Shaken, Satan Will Try to Place Great Fear Upon You!

More and more, you are going to hear about God's people going through trials and suffering all kinds of evil. And Satan will use those examples to try to convince you that God will not be there when you need Him—that He will not keep you from the wicked one!

We have been given great examples of faith under trial: According to church tradition, the apostle Paul was beheaded. Hebrews 11 lists the heroes of the faith who were burned at the stake, skinned alive, boiled in oil—all because they wouldn't recant their testimony of the Lord Jesus Christ.

Yet my message here is not meant to deal with why God's people suffer—why some are permitted to endure so much when His promises are so mighty. I don't know all the answers to that. But I do know that Paul said this: "For I reckon that the sufferings of this present time are not worthy to be compared with the glory which shall be revealed in us" (Romans 8:18).

Nothing can compare to the glory we look forward to! "If so be that we suffer with him [Christ], that we may be also glorified together" (verse 17).

I know also that God uses suffering to prepare us. We are going to go through economic suffering, sickness and other trials. I don't know why my wife, Gwen, has had cancer so many different times, or why my daughters Bonnie and Debbie have had cancer. I don't understand that kind of suffering.

But I do know this: If you aren't being prepared through trials, you will listen to the devil when he whispers to you, "God is not a Keeper of His people"—and you'll look for an easy ride to heaven! You'll run to some prosperity church to have your ears tickled. Then, when the first problem arises, you'll end up throwing away all your faith—because it hasn't answered your deepest problems and needs!

What was behind Judas' fall? How did this disciple become a traitor? This is important to know—because it gives us warning signs for our own lives, lest we stumble and fall too:

1. The Love of Money Had Taken Root in Judas' Heart!

"And he went his way, and communed with the chief priests and captains, how he might betray him unto them. And they were glad, and covenanted to give him money" (Luke 22:4-5).

The word "covenanted" here means "bargained." As Judas sat before these evil priests, he wouldn't settle for just fifteen or twenty pieces of silver—he had to have thirty or nothing. That was his bottom price!

Bible commentators make all kinds of excuses for Judas' betrayal. Many say that money was not his motive—that he only wanted to force Jesus to set up an earthly kingdom.

But the truth is, money was the motive! Why else would he bargain, arguing a price? He could have simply said, "Look, I only want Jesus forced into this position to make Him display His power"—and he would have taken any amount of silver. But the love of money had driven out of Judas' heart all the love he had for Jesus!

Indeed, the love of money is the root of all such evil (see 1 Timothy 6:10). It is the seed the devil plants in a man or woman's heart that drives out all love for Christ. Up sprouts the need to accumulate money. Then comes the need to count it and make sure it isn't lost. Afterward comes the need to build on it.

You may have set some goal for yourself—of retiring, or of being financially secure. I'm sure Judas had a financial goal too. But this kind never have enough—because the goal is always being lifted higher!

The devil tells you, "If you want to serve the Lord, wait till you get a certain amount in the bank. Then you'll be free to serve Him!" But after you get that much, Satan whispers: "That's really not enough, because interest rates are going down. You really need this much more...." And the figure keeps escalating!

Yet the Bible says:

"But they that will be rich fall into temptation and a snare, and into many foolish and hurtful lusts, which drown men in destruction and perdition. For the love of money is the root of all evil: which while some coveted after, they have erred [turned away] from the faith, and pierced themselves through with many sorrows. But thou, O man of God, flee these things" (1 Timothy 6:9-11).

If your life is focused on making a living—on the pursuit of money—then you have the very same spirit of Satan in you that Judas had in him! It was simple greed that turned Judas into a thief, a traitor and a murderer of Jesus Christ. And that proves Paul's argument that the love of money is the root and germ of all kinds of evil!

As you read this message, ask yourself: Have you sold out Christ in this way? Have you become a traitor to Him, bargaining your soul for more money?

There is nothing wrong with having a savings account. But if you have neglected Jesus because your life is wrapped up in accumulating money, then you too have sold out Jesus, as surely as Judas did!

2. Judas Became Blind to the Changes Overpowering Him!

Satan had dropped a veil over Judas' eyes, so he could not see how he had been changing. The disciple became blind to the evil and ruin that had settled into his heart.

Judas was familiar with the prophecies about the one coming who would betray the Redeemer. I wonder how many times he read or heard these words: "Mine own familiar friend, in whom I trusted, which did eat of my bread, hath lifted up his heel against me" (Psalm 41:9).

But never once did Judas think of himself as filling that awful role! "Me, the object of prophecy? Jeremiah and Isaiah saw my day? I'm not a betrayer of Christ—I am a simple disciple. I am not evil!"

Yet Jesus very clearly pointed a finger at the disciples and said, "But that the Scripture may be fulfilled, he that eateth bread with me hath lifted up his heel against me... one of you shall betray me" (John 13:18, 21). Was Judas so blind he could not see he was the man?

Today, we too read biblical prophecies that speak of our day. For example, Jesus said that in the last days many will again crucify Christ, putting Him to open shame, because they let their hearts grow cold: "Because iniquity shall abound, the love of many shall wax cold" (Matthew 24:12).

That prophecy was spoken hundreds of years ago. Yet I ask you: Is your heart cold toward the Lord today? Jesus said sin would abound everywhere—and the love of many believers would grow cold! Are you the man or woman whom this prophecy is putting its finger on right now?

Let me share with you the most shameful thing that can happen to those who once knew and loved Jesus: Without knowing it, they become the devil's last day "Judas statement"! If your love is growing cold, the devil will use you as his example—the same way he used Judas!

Satan will point you out to all the powers of hell, all the angels in glory and all who knew you on earth—and he'll say: "Look! He once walked with Jesus—and Jesus didn't keep him! Once again, I slipped into the Lord's flock and stole another lamb so close to Christ. I have his heart now, and I will ruin and destroy him. He proves by his falling away that God is not a Keeper!"

Nothing could be worse for you than to stand before the Lord and answer for all your friends and acquaintances, because you turned away from Him. You may say, "Don't put that burden on me—I'm only responsible for my own actions. I don't have to answer for anybody else!"

Not so! How many on your job once knew you as a lover of Jesus? You testified to them, you told them what Jesus did for you. They knew your walk with Christ.

But you turned your back on Him. And you've changed—yet you don't know you've changed, because the devil has blinded you! Day by day, week by week, year by year, you've become hardened in your heart.

Now all who once knew you as a lover of Jesus see a different person. And a crowd of witnesses will arise on Judgment Day and condemn you to the Judge: "You can't judge me, God, because I was looking at his life! Ten years ago he was on fire and loved You with all his heart. I was deep in sin—and yet I had my eye on him. I saw how close he was to You.

"Then he failed—and I thought, "What chance do I have?" Let my blood be upon him, Lord! What little hope I had of turning to You was taken from me by his failure to follow on!" That is how you become the Judas testimony!

Jesus Had the Last Word About His Keeping Power!

In His final prayer with His disciples, Jesus made His own statement—to heaven, hell and all mankind:

"Those that thou gavest me I have kept, and none of them is lost, but the son of perdition [Judas]; that the Scriptures might be fulfilled" (John 17:12).

Do you hear the truth of what Jesus is saying? "I lost only one—and I didn't really lose him, because he was of the devil from the beginning. I have kept everyone who has ever given Me his heart! I believe Judas could have been saved—because Jesus did everything He could for him. It wasn't God who hardened Judas' heart. He merely foresaw that Judas would harden himself to Christ, time after time. You see, Judas had a divided heart—and he chose not to repent! That is how he ended up as Satan's tool.

Hear the words well, dear saint: "Those that thou gavest me I have kept, and none of them is lost!" (John 17:12).

The example of Peter should encourage us. Jesus told him, "Peter, Satan is after you. He has desired to sift you, destroy you and turn you also into a traitor. But I'm praying for you, that your faith will not fail!"

Peter didn't fail in his faith—because Jesus kept him! Though he failed at the hour of temptation, he still had a heart that loved Christ—and Peter came back to Jesus, giving Him his heart and fully repenting. Jesus saw that hungry heart and said, "I'm going to keep you from the power of the devil!"

Beloved, God is going to keep you for "greater is he that is in you, than he that is in the world" (1 John 4:4). You can turn to Psalm 91 and believe every verse about His protection over you. You may go through a season of suffering, but nobody can touch your peace with God!

We can't know what tomorrow holds—but I pray that as believers we can each say with Job, "Though he slay me, yet will I trust in him" (Job 13:15). And I know for sure if the Lord does let His wall of protection down, it's for a reason. We may never understand it all. But we can know this: "He that keepeth thee will not sleep" (Psalm 121:3).

It is true and it is sure: He "is able to keep you from falling, and present you faultless before the presence of his glory with exceeding joy" (Jude 24).

Hallelujah!

— David Wilkerson was the founding pastor of Times Square Church in New York City. There he ministered to gang members and drug addicts. In 1971, he founded World Challenge, Inc., which supports missionaries and outreaches throughout the world. He died in 2011.

Reprinted by permission: World Challenge, Inc., PO Box 260, Lindale, TX 75771. http://worldchallenge.org

LESSON 6

DECISIONS—STAGE ONE

MAIN PRINCIPLE

As we see Jesus pray in anguish in the Garden of Gethsemane and allow Himself to be arrested, we need to decide if we are willing to follow in Jesus' footsteps.

Are we willing to follow Jesus and put our relationship with the Father first in our lives, even if it means going toward the cross and laying down everything for our Lord?

OUR FIRST PRIORITY

by Harry Schroeder

There is something lacking in our devotional life today. I've seen it manifested again and again. It's that most of us don't consider spending private, intimate time with God our highest priority. Sitting in the private place of God hasn't become the single, most important thing we could ever contemplate.

More than ever, God is calling us to settle this issue in our lives. God has called us to a high and a holy calling. He is offering us a life filled with His dynamic power. A life filled with His richness and His abundance; a life of purpose. But we get side-tracked—there are too many things that clamor for our attention. Actually only a few are important.

Panoramically, as we look at the church, we see the problem. It is engrossed in too many of the elementary things of life. God wants to take us to the mountains but we can't get our feet out of the mud.

The writer of Hebrews tells us to set aside every weight and encumbrance that besets us. Many things try to trip us and keep us from fulfilling the great destiny that God has for us.

One of them is our complacency. Complacency has slowly eroded the church. It seems as though the devil has been wooing us to sleep. Materialism grabs at the heart of the church in America. Passivity and materialism both are creeping into the church because there is a lack of worship life in the church. By that, I'm not referring to our Sunday morning music, but to a realistic lifestyle of worship.

Many times when we hear the word of God taught to us we think that somehow, some day we can "arrive." We hope to finally come to where we are really "spiritual." Yet, this is a misunderstanding of the ways of God.

We have to realize that we will always need God. Most of the church really doesn't believe that. They believe in God but they never really rely on His strength.

The problem in our marriages, our homes and our work places isn't caused by a blaring television. It isn't a result of secular humanism in the schools. It isn't because there is abortion in the land. The problem is, Christians don't sit in the private place with God. We have hearts that are cold to the ways of God. We have hearts that are weak when they ought to be strong. Why? Because we are not spending time before God and letting His presence, His values, and His heart touch our hearts.

> APART FROM THE PRESENCE OF GOD, WE ARE AS WEAK AND AS POWERLESS AS ANYBODY IN THE WORLD.

Changed by Him

As we sit in the presence of God, His grace begins to permeate our souls. His presence will begin to change us. But we must make the commitment to come before Him. We can memorize the Bible, go to church meetings, know all the doctrines and trends, but until we begin to allow God Himself to change us we are not going to reach the fullness of our potential.

In addition to that, when we spend time with God, His power begins to move in our lives and renews us. I spent years praying, "Lord, change this person," or "Lord, help that person to get his life together." God finally said to me, "Take it easy. Why don't you just sit with Me for a while and let Me work on you? I want to change YOU."

It's just like the time when I first met the Lord. I grew up in the Baptist church and I thought I was saved. I had answered every altar call that had been given. But then one night, I went to a Bible study and during a time of prayer at the end I prayed, "Lord, save my cousin." For the first time I heard the voice of God speak to me. He said, "What about you?" "Me?" I thought. "I'm Baptist. How could I not be saved?"

Many times that's the way we are in our prayer time. We beat down the devil for everybody else but never sit with God and let Him change us, and let Him cause our hearts to be warmed by His presence.

I'm not saying to quit reading your Bible. As a matter of fact, you should take your Bible with you when you pray. Read it in the presence of God. Many times I open my Bible and say, "God, cause these words to speak to me. They're just words on a page unless you breathe life into them. Please, open my heart, Lord. I want to be changed today as I read." Read your Bible in the presence of God.

Occasionally in Paul's epistles he says, "I'm telling you this in the presence of God." I always wondered what that meant. Then I realized that he was coming out of the place of prayer where God was communing with him. There was an exchange of life between him and God. From that vantage point God was able to speak through him truths and oracles that would shape people's lives.

Intimacy and Reality in Our Prayer Life

The woman who had the issue of blood had had it for eighteen years. She had endured much at the hands of doctors, yet one day she came to Jesus and touched the hem of His garment and was healed. I believe the greatest weakness of the church today is that we don't touch God. We have to get beyond, "Now I lay me down to sleep." God wants us to have intimacy and reality with Him in our prayer life.

Apart from that there isn't any Christianity. It's like trying to be a Christian without Christ. Apart from the presence of God we are as weak and as powerless as anybody in the world.

In John 15:5, Jesus said, "Apart from Me you can do nothing." He was talking to the apostles. If they couldn't do anything without Jesus, how much more do we need Him? We need to spend serious, quality time with God. How blessed we would be if we would make it our highest priority.

When the people came to Jesus and asked what the greatest commandment was, He said it was to love God more than everything else. This is still the command that God is issuing forth. He's looking for a people that will love Him with all their hearts. He's not mad if that's not where we are spiritually, but He wants us to move on. What God really wants is a people who passionately know Him, and who are passionately joined to Him.

Maintaining a Firm Foundation

If we miss that concept, then our attempts to be a salesman or an evangelist won't work. Why? Because we haven't settled the first issue of why we are doing what we are doing. There are so many things today that God is calling His people to be a part of, but until we settle the number one issue, the rest of them have no foundation.

Are there ever times in your life when you really seem to be getting your "spiritual act" together and then suddenly it falls apart again? That happens because there is no firm foundation. Realize that the foundation is not an understanding of creation or the virgin birth or even spiritual warfare. A true foundation in your life is settling the issue of loving God first and foremost. Everything else depends on it.

We put people on pedestals if their first priority in all things is the Lord. But God says that is just the entry level into His kingdom. If you love God with all your heart then you have a foundation on which to build. We sometimes ask, "Lord, why don't the sick get well when I pray for them?" God says, "It is because you are operating without a firm foundation." We need to take care of that.

In II Corinthians 11:2, it says, "For I am jealous for you with a godly jealousy; for I betrothed you to one husband, that to Christ I might present you as a pure virgin." God's desire for His body is that we would be offered to Him a pure virgin kept only for Him.

In the book of Numbers when the Israelites came into the promised land, they divided the land for "their inheritance." God said the priests and the Levites didn't get anything physically because their inheritance was the Lord Himself. Today, we are the priests that God has called who are to receive Him as our inheritance. Our lives are to be joined to Him— not to the things of this world.

Called as Kings

God has also called us to be kings. Deuteronomy 17:17 says that a king should not acquire gold and silver for himself. The Lord didn't want the king's heart to be caught up in riches. It is the spirit of the world that causes us to race after money.

That doesn't mean it is bad to be rich. If the Lord blesses you, praise Him for it. Just don't let the money become your focus. We need to get our eyes off the things that the world calls important and put our focus on that which God calls important.

"But I am afraid, lest as the serpent deceived Eve by his craftiness, your minds should be led astray from the simplicity and the purity of devotion to Christ" (II Corinthians 11:3). Paul was saying here, "I'm afraid that you are going to be tripped up like Eve was."

The devil went to Eve and said, "If you eat this fruit, you can become like God." Eve ate the fruit to find an easy way to be like God. Her desire wasn't to be godly; it was to look like she was. She wanted to have the goods without the reality.

There is too much of this in the church. "Buy this CD. Send for this book. You will be like this." But the truth is, those things are only tools that we can learn from. What God has called us to be, first and foremost, is a people who will spend time in the private place with Him.

At our church I realized that what I say on Sunday is almost irrelevant unless people sit down afterwards and find God themselves. That is the truth. I have no delusions about being an incredible speaker on Sunday mornings. I am no more dynamic with a microphone on Sunday morning than I am Monday evening talking to my wife at home.

Get Serious with God

We have to look beyond the impact of great speakers and fantastic teachers. We need to get serious with God and let Him form our hearts. We cannot be a people lusting after every trend that comes through the church simply because we think that trend is going to answer our need. The answer is God Himself, found and understood in the secret place and in His word.

Deuteronomy 17:18 says that whenever a new king came in he was supposed to write for himself a copy of the laws of God. He was to get a copy of the law, write it down word for word, and read it so that it would cause his heart to fear and love God. We, too, should study His scriptures in the light of His presence.

We are all familiar with the story of Job. Every one of his children was killed. All of his property was destroyed. All of his livestock was killed. In one hour he lost everything.

But Job 1:20 says, "Then Job arose and tore his robe and shaved his head, and he fell to the ground and worshipped." I don't know about you, but that confused me. I read that and thought, "That doesn't make sense." That he arose and tore his robe was normal because he was in mourning. That he "shaved his head" was understandable because he was in grief.

But when he "fell to the ground," I would have used another word instead of "worshipped." Maybe something like, "moaned," or "cried out to God," or "was bitter." Yet, Job didn't do any of those things. He <u>worshipped</u>. There was a reality deep within Job of the relationship that he had with his God.

It would be very easy for him to be cynical or mad. But instead, his first response was to worship God. Most of us respond to anything negative with, "God, why is this happening?" We rebuke the devil or get upset. When was the last time something horrible happened and you fell down and worshipped?

God is calling us to be such a people; people who will respond this way. It's a supernatural lifestyle. It can't be done unless God does it in us; unless the grace of God begins to form that kind of heart in us.

That is how Christianity works. We will miss much of the work of God in our lives if we don't sit alone with Him and allow Him to say, "You messed up today." We've got to sit in His presence so that He can commune with us and teach us.

For me, at the beginning, it would have been more convenient to have read a book, listened to a CD or gone to a seminar than to sit for hours before God. It's a lot easier to do those things. But to sit before God, just listening for His voice, is more difficult because we're not used to it. Yet, God has called us to be real with Him every day. Soon, it starts getting easier and better.

In Psalm 27:4, David says, "One thing I have asked the Lord, that I shall seek: that I may dwell in the house of the Lord all the days of my life, to behold the beauty of the Lord, and meditate in His temple." David, the Bible says, was a man after God's own heart. The one thing that he desired above all else was to be with the Lord all the time. The passion of our hearts should be to desire to spend time seeking and worshipping God, and doing what He tells us.

The chorus of a prophetic song entitled "Spending Time" by Steve Urspringer summarizes what I'm saying:

Jesus said,
"If you would spend time with Me
Like you do with your TV
Or the movies that you see
Then your burdens I would bear,
Your problems I would share,
If you would wait on Me;
If you would spend time with Me."

The final chorus is even more pointed:

Jesus said,
"If you would spend time with Me
Like you do with your TV
Then the crippled and the lame
Would respond to My name
If you would wait on Me;
If you would spend time with Me."

Let's spend time with Him.

©1995 Priesthood Publications

— Harry Schroeder is a pastor at Southgate Church (Victory Fellowship) in St. Louis. He also works with the youth and is a basketball announcer.

Reprinted with permission: Psalmist Magazine.

LESSON 7

HUMILIATION—STAGE TWO

MAIN PRINCIPLE

As we read of Jesus silently enduring being mocked, spat upon and beaten, we realize that He suffered this humiliation for our sake. He did this so that we would be able to come into the fullness of relationship with Him. Are we willing to stand firm in our belief in Jesus, desire only His approval, and endure humiliation for Him?

ASSIGNED ARTICLE

FILL US WITH YOUR PASSION, LORD!

by Kent Henry

I'm currently finding my heart's cry in this statement: "Lord, fill us with Your passion. Let us know Your zeal and strength to do your work and will." The church is overdue for a passion/zeal transplant. I'm not referring to strengthening your own passion or zeal for the things of God, but asking God for a renewed deposit of His zeal.

The scriptures are very clear about the zeal of the Lord of Hosts. This is the power of the living God to accomplish the word and work He has called into being.

"And the surviving remnant of the house of Judah shall again take root downward and bear fruit upward. For out of Jerusalem shall go forth a remnant, and out of Mount Zion survivors (those who escape). The zeal of the Lord of hosts shall perform this." (Is. 37:31, 32).

The Zeal Of The Lord Of Hosts

Consider the power and the might it will take to establish the root downward and the fruit upward; it is truly an awesome thing. Our Lord of Hosts has a certain zeal about Him. There is a certain passion and strength within the God of heaven to bring to pass those things He has willed.

This is the zeal I wish to tap into. This is the zeal I want to run forward in. This is the inexhaustible supply of the strength of God. And this is the passion contained inherently in the Holy Spirit who lives inside of us when we decide to flow in it.

"Yes, truth is lacking; and he who turns aside from evil makes himself a prey. Now the Lord saw and it was displeasing in His sight that there was no justice. And He saw that there was no man and was astonished that there was no one to intercede; then His own arm brought salvation to Him and His righteousness upheld Him. And He put on righteousness like a breastplate and a helmet of salvation on His head; and He put on garments of vengeance for clothing, and wrapped Himself with *zeal as a mantle.*" (Is. 59:15-17)

Zeal As A Mantle

Zeal as a mantle: now here is a revelation! Put on the garment (mantle) of praise for the spirit of heaviness (fainting), but don't forget about putting on the zeal of the Lord as a mantle either. The strength of God and the spirit of might is equal to the work and will your Father has placed upon you.

Some of us are growing weak or feeling desperate as it seems as if there is no strength left within us to do His work. First, we must reconsider where we are spending our time: are we working for the Lord or with Him. I think many of us have had days, weeks and months where we were very busy, but it was doing our thing or just things that were low priorities concerning the heart of God.

Some of us have let doing good things become the enemy of doing great things, and great things became the enemy of doing God's thing. Therefore, we have spent tons of our own strength and energy going down mistaken paths for long periods of time. "Lord, restore the years that the locust and cankerworm have eaten away." (Joel 2:25)

Secondly, we need to redefine how we are doing the

things God sets before us. Is it according to wisdom and the efficiency of God's spirit realm? Or is it in our own strength and masterplanning? Or is it really through Christ who will continually strengthen us as we rely on Him?

Zealous To Repent

The book of Revelation records the admonition and rebuke of the Lord Jesus to the Laodicean church for their lack of passion and fire toward God. And here was His advice: "I advise you to buy (purchase) from Me gold refined by fire, that you may become rich, and white garments, that you may clothe yourself, and that the shame of your nakedness may not be revealed and eye salve to anoint your eyes, that you may see. Those whom I love, I reprove and discipline; *be zealous* therefore, and *repent.*" (Rev. 3:18, 19).

Be zealous and repent. Here is a directive everyone can hear and do. If nothing else, please at least be zealous and repent of the old habits and patterns to flow anew in the strength, zeal and passion of the Lord. I'm closing with the words to a new song the Lord transmitted to me at the close of a prayer meeting where I was considering these very things.

Where are the people of passion?
Where are the people who care?
Where are those who will steal away, find God in the secret lair?
Where are the people of fire?
Where are the people with zeal?

Where are those with a Jesus heart, and hands that really heal?

We are the people, people of holiness,
We are the people, people of righteousness,
We are the people, people of zeal and fire,
We are the people, people of God's desire.

We are the people with minstrel hearts.
We are the people of song.
We are the people with psalmist voice,
Singing the Father's Song.

We are the people of heaven's grace.
We are the people who share,
His passion and zeal to touch the world,
Displaying His holy care.

It's still our choice. I want to be a part of a generation that is recorded in heavenly history as possessing a heart of wisdom and a heart of zeal. We just can't be denied.

—Kent Henry is a traveling singer and songwriter who teaches and uses praise with prayer and worship and intercession. He is currently also involved in the leadership of Destiny Church of St. Louis.

Reprinted by permission: *Psalmist Magazine.*

PSALM 77—ARE YOU LISTENING, GOD?

by Rev. John F. Stocker

Psalm 77 is the heart cry of a godly man who has seen his nation forget and forsake God. He has seen that nation devastated— in the process of being destroyed—and now his heart is aching and he is crying out to God. He has said, *"God do something about this situation."* Yet nothing seems to get done. Here we have an example that we can all relate to because we have all been in a situation where we prayed and cried out to God without getting an answer. In addition to God not answering our prayer, the comfort of the Holy Spirit has even been withdrawn. After praying and not having our prayer answered we become frustrated— sometimes even angry with God.

According to our theology, this is when the Holy Spirit is supposed to come and wrap his arms around us and comfort us. Every one of us has probably experienced a time when we did experience the comfort of the Holy Spirit. However, we can also look back and say there have been times we have not experienced His comfort. Sometimes we've been hurting so bad we didn't think we could survive.

In Psalm 77, Asaph is experiencing these same frustrations. Psalm 77:1, *"I cried unto God with my voice, even unto God with my voice; and he gave ear unto me."* Every time you see this kind of repetition in the scriptures (he says *"with his voice"* twice), the writer is trying to emphasize a point. Asaph was crying on an ongoing basis. He just cried and cried and cried unto God with his voice. The

second part of the verse, *"and he gave ear unto me"* plants a seed of hope.

Now we think, *"Praise God, we are getting some place."* The Lord gave ear unto him. But if you continue to read this Psalm you don't find any place where God ever did anything. It's worse to know that God hears, yet doesn't do anything. You would probably feel better about the whole deal if you knew He *didn't* hear. If you could say, *"God is hard of hearing, or not around today because He's on vacation,"* it wouldn't be so bad. But to be down here pouring your heart out to God knowing that He is up there—hears you—and is not doing a thing about it—can really bug you. This makes God look bad, doesn't it?

Vs 2, *"In the day of my trouble I sought the Lord. My sore ran in the night, and ceased not: my soul refused to be comforted."* The word *"refused"* makes me think maybe there was an attempt by the Holy Spirit to comfort Asaph. At times I have seen people who *refused* to be comforted.

A good example can be someone who has lost a loved one. After a time of grieving, that person must make a conscious decision to go forward with their life. Perhaps the grieving person feels that letting go of their grief means they didn't love that person as much as they should have. Maybe they have become accustomed to the extra attention and comfort of the people around them. It's an individual situation for each person experiencing it.

Sometimes our grief is so great that in essence we *refuse* to be comforted. We make up our mind. We don't care what anybody says to us. We don't care what God

> THIS PSALM COULD HAVE BEEN
> WRITTEN TODAY.

says to us. We are not going to be comforted, period. Instead of comfort we want answers. Isn't the Bible practical? This is Asaph's situation. He doesn't want comfort; he wants answers to his prayers.

Vs. 3, "*I remembered God, and was troubled: I complained, and my spirit was overwhelmed.*" "*Complained*" literally means, "*to converse with one's self.*" If you choose to go this way, fine, but God will not have anything to do with it. Bellyaching and whining to God does absolutely no good because He sees everything about the situation. It is unproductive to whine to God. The result in Asaph's situation was that his spirit was overwhelmed.

For some people whining will be a hard habit to break because it has been a way of life for them. Every time something doesn't go right, they are questioning God, "*Why don't you do this, and why did you do that?*" This attitude will not lead to victory in anyone's life.

Vs. 4, "*Thou holdest mine eyes waking: I am so troubled that I cannot speak.*" He accuses God of not letting him sleep. It's usually a lack of faith and trust, laying there worrying, that keeps us awake at night.

Vs. 5-6, "*I have considered the days of old, the years of ancient times. I call to remembrance my song in the night: I communed with mine own heart: and my spirit made diligent search.*" This tactic is one a lot of us try in this situation. We have all been taught to think back to the good things the Lord has done in the past.

Vs. 7, "*Will the Lord cast off forever? And will he be favorable no more? Is his mercy clean gone forever? Doth his promise fail for evermore? Hath God forgotten to be gracious? Hath he in anger shut up his tender mercies?*" After Asaph attempts to remember God's faithfulness, he comes back to the fact that God is not answering his prayer right then.

Like Asaph, it IS good for us to look back to the good things from the past, but sooner or later, we all come back to the old question of "*So what?*" Yesterday's victories and answers don't help us today. We need answers for today's problems today. Eventually, we have to deal with our unanswered prayers. We ask, "*What is going on here God? God, what has happened to you? Has your mercy and grace changed? Have you just gotten angry and written us off forever?*"

Vs. 10-20, "*I said, This is my infirmity: but I will remember the years of the right hand of the Most High. I will remember the works of the Lord: surely I will remember thy wonders of old. I will meditate also of all thy work, and talk of thy doings. Thy way, O God, is in the sanctuary: who is so great a God as our God? Thou art the God that doest wonders: thou hast declared thy strength among the people. Thou hast with thine arm redeemed thy people, the sons of Jacob and Joseph. Selah. The waters saw thee, O God, the waters saw thee; they were afraid: the depths also were troubled. The clouds poured out water: the skies sent out a sound: thine arrows also went abroad. The voice of thy thunder was in the heaven: the lightnings lightened the world: the earth trembled and shook. Thy way is in the sea, and thy path in the great waters, and thy footsteps are not known. Thou leadest thy people like a flock by the hand of Moses and Aaron.*"

Now, he does two things that we often do. Once again, they are good things to do. First, he goes back to remembering again. Then, he starts confessing the right things. Today, this is what many of us have been taught to do. We figure we can move God by just confessing the right things.

This Psalm could have been written today [updated]. I have walked and lived it all. I have experienced every bit of it. First I tried remembering and I still got frustrated. Then, I try confessing that God is good and going to take care of it all. It's all in this Psalm. But, the problem is when Asaph gets done, God still hasn't done anything.

Remembering the goodness of God and confessing the things you believe are good things to do. However, there are times when all of your praying, standing, confessing and remembering will not move God.

There is a key here in the thirteenth verse. "Thy way, O God, is in the sanctuary." First, he admits that he doesn't understand what is happening. His prayers, confession and faith aren't working. Even the Holy Spirit doesn't seem to be working in his life. He realizes he doesn't understand God's ways. Then, he realizes that to understand and know God's ways, he will have to go into the sanctuary.

What exactly IS the "*sanctuary?*"

WHAT EXACTLY IS THE "SANCTUARY"?

We begin to understand that in the Old Testament the sanctuary is the place where the beauty, strength, majesty, righteousness and holiness of Almighty God is displayed. In the sanctuary you see His divine supernatural ways. After you have confessed, stood in faith, prayed, cried—done everything the teachers have taught you to do—with no results—God says, "*Draw nigh unto me and come into my sanctuary.*"

What is the sanctuary today? It's the place where you encounter Him and His ways will be known to you. Many of us have the problem of wanting the answer without wanting to encounter Him in His sanctuary. We are content to let God be our errand boy. Some of us go through our whole life treating God like that, until one day God says, "*No.*" We are walking along and all of a sudden the slack is pulled out of our leash, leaving us standing there griping and complaining to God.

If we have been living our life without any tight fellowship, communion or relationship with God, we won't know His ways. Then, when God says, "*Honey, this ain't going to fly anymore,*" that is it. We can stand and complain all we want to, but we will never understand God's reasoning.

Some people never understand God's ways because they refuse to go to the sanctuary. They never get to the place where His glory, holiness, majesty, righteousness and His ways are revealed.

PRAYER WILL NEVER REPLACE REPENTANCE.

After we've complained and accused God of being unfair, and then finally go to the sanctuary in desperation, within about thirty seconds, it is like the scales fall off our eyes. Suddenly we are saying, "*Oh, God, I don't believe what I have been saying and doing.*"

This is like Job's encounter with God. Job's encounter lasted longer than thirty seconds, going from Job Chapter 37 to 42.

Chapter 38:1, (and I give you Pastor John's translation) "*Then the Lord answered Job out of the whirlwind, and said, 'Who is this jerk that has been shooting off his mouth while having absolutely no knowledge whatsoever of what he was talking about.'*" Read the book of Job. Job is walking around from the very beginning saying, "*I am a sinless man, I am perfect. There is nothing wrong with me.*" Back in chapters 9 and 10 he accuses God of unfaithfulness. He basically says, "*I wish He (God) were a man so that I could get him face to face, eyeball to eyeball and have it out.*" Don't ever talk like that!

In Chapter 38, God has had enough. God shows up and He starts in by saying, "*Job, I am going to ask you some questions, and I want you to answer me.*" Chapters 38, 39, 40, 41 and into 42 are where God is just letting Job have it. "*Where were you when I created all of this? Where were you when I hung the stars out there? Where were you when I created all of those animals? Hey, did I consult with you about how to feed them all? Would you like to have that task just one day, to have to provide for all the animals on this earth?*"

Job doesn't have any answers. Finally, God says, "*Well, speak up!*" Job answers, "*I think I have said too much already.*" Finally, in Chapter 42, when God is done with the interrogation, Job responds. Job 42:1-4, "*Then Job answered the Lord, and said, I know that thou canst do everything, and that no thought can be withholden from thee. Who is he that hideth counsel without knowledge? Therefore have I uttered that I understood not; things too wonderful for me, which I knew not. Hear, I beseech thee, and I will speak: I will demand of thee, and declare thou unto me.*"

In other words, instead of telling You how to run the universe, I am just going to ask what you want to do with my life? That is all I am going to ask. After he goes into the SANCTUARY he says, Vs. 5, "*I have heard of thee by the hearing of the ear; but now mine eye seeth thee.*" (In God's presence Job saw the righteousness, holiness, majesty and awe of God. Immediately his attitude changes.) Vs. 6, "*Wherefore I abhor myself, and REPENT in dust and ashes.*"

What about Asaph's situation? If the nation had repented instead of complaining, they would have been delivered instantly. God could have done like He did when Sennacherib's host came, and all those tens of thousands died.

Here is a key concept I want you to grasp. Prayer will never replace repentance. If you are not seeing answers to your prayers, one of the first things you should do is go to God and say, "*God, let me come into your sanctuary. Shine the light of your purity and holiness on me. See if there be in me some wicked way that hinders my prayers.*" This is absolutely necessary to see our prayers answered.

If you feel like God just doesn't answer your prayers and everyone treats you terribly, ask God how He sees your situation. Ask Him to show you all the ways that you have been messing it up. If you have been complaining to Him, you can't be hearing from Him. Human beings cannot talk and listen effectively at the same time. Go to His sanctuary, quiet yourself for a while and let God talk to you. Then do what He tells you to do.

"*Thy way O Lord is in the sanctuary.*" Go to the sanctuary. I guarantee that you will NOT like what He tells you, but it WILL set you free. Why don't we like God's counsel—because HIS way is in the sanctuary. "*Even as the heavens are high above the earth, so are my ways and my thoughts higher than your ways and your thoughts saith the Lord.*" In the sanctuary we learn to trust Him. When we do it God's way, we find out God shows up on the scene. He then answers our prayers.

—John Stocker founded Resurrection Fellowship in Loveland, CO in 1983. He was the senior pastor there until he retired in 2010.

Reprinted by permission: Rev. John F. Stocker

LESSON 8

OUR CHOICE—STAGES THREE AND FOUR

MAIN PRINCIPLE

We must choose to avoid pride and hardness of heart and keep our hearts pliable towards the Lord. We need to choose to let go of our sinful attitudes and actions when God reveals them to us. As we truly repent of our sins and turn to Jesus, we will receive the help and forgiveness we need.

THE MARVELOUS BENEFITS OF REPENTANCE!

by David Wilkerson

I want to talk to you about two very important aspects of repentance:

1. What it requires, and
2. Its marvelous benefits!

The longer I walk with Jesus, the more I am convinced repentance is not just for sinners, but also for believers. It is not simply a one-time thing, but something God's people are called to do until Jesus returns.

And I hope to show you that every Christian who maintains a repentant attitude brings upon his life God's special attention. Indeed, repentance opens up something to us that nothing else can. If we walk before the Lord with a repentant heart, we will be inundated with incredible blessings!

But for now, I want to tell you what I believe is absolutely necessary to obtaining a repentant heart. First of all, this type of heart is soft and pliable. It responds to and acts upon godly reproof. It is tender, easily molded by the Holy Spirit.

But the number-one characteristic of a repentant heart—its absolute foundation—is a readiness to acknowledge guilt! It is a willingness to accept blame for wrongdoing—to say, "I am the one, Lord. I have sinned!"

You see, if there is no admitting to sin, there can be no repentance: **"For godly sorrow worketh repentance to salvation not to be repented of..."** (2 Corinthians 7:10). If you're not willing to acknowledge you're wrong, you're saying you don't need to repent. You see yourself as having done no wrong in the sight of God.

Before Pilate released Jesus into the hands of murderous priests and elders, he wanted the world to know it wasn't his fault. So he called for a basin of water, dipped his hands into it and absolved himself before the angry mob. He declared himself innocent of Christ's blood:

"When Pilate saw that he could prevail nothing, but that rather a tumult was made, he took water, and washed his hands before the multitude, saying, I am innocent of the blood of this just person: see ye to it" (Matthew 27:24).

The phrase "See ye to it" here means, "Make sure you all know my hands are clean. I have done nothing wrong. I am clean from all guilt!"

Of course, Pilate's hands were not clean; he was about to hand over the Son of God to murderers. This kind of thinking shuts a person off from any possibility of repentance. Had a prophet approached Pilate the next day, preaching, "Repent or perish!" the ruler would have been aghast. "Who, me?" he'd have said. "I've done nothing wrong. I have washed my hands of everything. How can I repent when I haven't sinned?"

John writes: **"If we say that we have no sin, we deceive ourselves, and the truth is not in us.... If we** say that we have not sinned, we make him a liar, and his word is not in us" (1 John 1:8, 10).

Now, I was raised in the church, and during my life-time I have seen many churches split in two. Each party would make an enemy of the other, until finally one group would leave and move down the road to start another church. Then the two parties would hurl curses at each other, gossiping, ridiculing, spreading vicious rumors.

If you were to listen to the justifications each party made, you'd be amazed that no one is to blame. No Christian on either side admits to any wrongdoing. Instead, they look on each other as "the enemy" and wait for God to curse and judge them. They say to their opponents, "You just wait. When people in your church start dropping dead, then you'll know who's right!"

It goes on for years! They all claim God is on their side, and they encourage themselves with Bible passages they find to fit their agenda. In essence, they wash their hands, claiming, "I have done no wrong!" "

But the truth is, both groups anger the Lord. Like Pilate, neither is in a position to repent—so they end up under His wrath! They become a congregation of the dead, living in a spiritual wilderness. Their families are troubled. They are always at odds with themselves. And it's all because nobody will accept any blame! No one says, "I'm the one who needs to be dealt with. I need prayer!"

The Prophet Malachi Was Shocked and Grieved by the Spiritual Blindness of God's People in His Day!

Malachi was a prophet sent by God to reprove Israel. Yet each time he went to the people with a strong message, they reacted with mock innocence.

The first time Malachi came to them, he preached, "You have profaned the holiness of the Lord! You know how to weep and cover the altar with your tears. But God has rejected all your sacrifices—because you're in sin!"

The people reacted with total shock. They answered, "But, why? What have we done wrong?"

Malachi answered: **"...the Lord...regardeth not the offering any more, or receiveth it with good will at your hand. Ye say, Wherefore? Because the Lord hath been witness between thee and the wife of thy youth, against whom thou hast dealt treacherously..."** (Malachi 2:13-14).

Their sin was they had been divorcing their wives and marrying heathen women. And all the while they had continued going to the altar, performing all the religious activities, with their hearts full of sin. These men had openly rebelled against God's commands. But they denied it to themselves, saying, "What are you saying? We're clean!"

So Malachi came to them a second time, preaching: **"Ye have wearied the Lord with your words..."** (Malachi 2:17). In other words: "You are saying things that have absolutely shocked God. Your profanities have wearied Him!"

Again, the people responded with mock innocence: **"...Wherein have we wearied him?..."** (same verse). They said, in essence, "How could we have wearied God? We've done no wrong."

Malachi answered: **"...When ye say, Every one that doeth evil is good in the sight of the Lord, and he delighteth in them; or, Where is the God of judgment?"** (same verse).

You see, the people had been encouraging evildoers in the congregation. They knew full well that these rebels were in sin—but they assured them all would be well, that no judgment would fall on them. Simply put, they were blunting God's message—calling evil good, and good evil. Yet they said to Malachi, "Why are you saying this? We are innocent of any wrongdoing."

Again Malachi came back to them, this time crying: "You have robbed God!" And again the people answered with their stock response: "What do you mean? How have we robbed God?"

Malachi answered: **"...In tithes and offerings"** (Malachi 3:8). He said, "You bring only garbage to the Lord's altar! You offer animals for sacrifice that are lame, blind and halt. These aren't the tithes and offerings that belong to God. You are robbing Him of your best!"

Finally, Malachi gave up preaching to them because they wouldn't hear him. The final chapter of this book tells us he bypassed them all and turned to a small, discerning, repentant remnant. These people received his reproof, and their hearts were moved by the Spirit of God. They acted on Malachi's convicting words—and in turn God blessed them mightily!

How Different David's Attitude Was From the Mock-Innocent Hearers!

David continually searched his heart before God. He was quick to cry, "I've sinned, Lord. I stand in need of prayer!" **"I acknowledged my sin unto thee, and mine iniquity have I not hid. I said, I will confess my transgressions unto the Lord; and thou forgavest the iniquity of my sin..."** (Psalm 32:5).

Being repentant doesn't mean you simply try to make things right with the person you've wronged. No—it's about making things right with God! God is the One who has been sinned against. Yes, we are to apologize to our brothers and sisters whenever we wrong them. But, more importantly, we are to repent of our sin before God. David said:

"For I acknowledge my transgressions: and my sin is ever before me. Against thee, thee only, have I sinned, and done this evil in thy sight: that thou mightest be justified when thou speakest, and be clear when thou judgest" (Psalm 51:3-5).

David believed in conducting heart searchings—in the hard discipline of digging out sin in his heart: **"Search me, O God, and know my heart: try me, and know my thoughts: And see if there be any wicked way in me, and lead me in the way everlasting"** (Psalm 139:23-24).

This man continually opened up his heart to God's searchlight. He said, "Lord, come and examine every corner of my life. If I've sinned against You in any way and I don't know it, please—reveal it to me. I repent!"

Perhaps you search your heart as well. Yet you come away from the Spirit's dealings saying, "Thank goodness, I'm clean. I don't have any sin in me." Beloved, you are deceived! Scripture says that *all* have sinned and fallen short of God's glory: **"I the Lord search the heart, I try the reins [test the emotions], even to give every man according to his ways, and according to the fruit of his doings"** (Jeremiah 17:10).

Isaiah confessed: **"For our transgressions are multiplied before thee, and our sins testify against us: for our transgressions are with us; and as for our iniquities, we know them"** (Isaiah 59:12). The prophet was saying, "We know all about our own sins!" Of course God knows when we say or do wrong things. But we know it too!

What are these known transgressions Isaiah was talking about? They are; **"...lying against the Lord, and departing away from our God, speaking oppression and revolt, conceiving and uttering from the heart words of falsehood"** (Isaiah 59:13).

There is one sin from this list we all find easy to justify—and that is "uttering from the heart words of falsehood." This means telling others something you've heard that you believe to be true, yet in fact it is false. You may utter it "from the heart"—yet there's no getting around its falsehood!

Some Christians think they can say virtually anything about anyone as long as they're sincere about it. They reason, "I mean no harm in saying it. It may not be what others think, but I believe it's true with all my heart."

Yet, what if a word from a well-meaning heart is a lie? How could any Christian justify saying it? How could anyone think, "My hands are clean"? Even if some damaging piece of information that's spoken is true, it is truth that has fallen to the ground and been trampled in mud! **"Talk no more so exceeding proudly; let not arrogancy come out of your mouth: for the Lord is a God of knowledge, and by him actions are weighed"** (1 Samuel 2:3).

God knows—and we know—all about our sinful tongues. And He will not tolerate gossip or slander in any form!

Those Whom God Uses Are Very Sensitive to Their Own Sins and They Grieve Over Sins in the Body of Christ!

Ezra was a godly scribe who loved the law of God and walked circumspectly before Him. He also was a great prayer warrior and a faithful preacher of God's Word. It would be hard to believe this man would need to repent of any sin.

But Ezra's heart broke over all the compromise he witnessed among God's people. When he went to Jerusalem, he saw uncleanness, idolatry, mixed marriages. Of course, none of it was his sin—yet he didn't boast, "Everybody around me may be backsliding, but my heart is right before God!" No! Instead, Ezra cast himself on the ground, weeping and confessing as if the people's sins were his own. He identified himself with God's people—and he shared their shame!

"...Ezra...prayed, and...confessed, weeping and casting himself down before the house of God... he did eat no bread, nor drink water: for he mourned because of the transgression of them that had been carried away" (Ezra 10:1, 6).

"...I fell upon my knees, and spread out my hands unto the Lord my God, and said, O my God, I am ashamed and blush to lift up my face to thee, my God: for our iniquities are increased over our head, and our trespass is grown up unto the heavens" (Ezra 9:5-6)

Ezra confessed not only his own weakness, but the sins of the whole congregation. He mourned, wept and felt the hurt of sin that had spread throughout God's house. I ask you: Do you take repentance that seriously?

Daniel had the same kind of repentant heart. He was a righteous man of prayer and devotion who lived so holy, you wouldn't expect to find him repenting. But Daniel's heart was sensitive to sin—and he too identified with the people's horrible sins: **"O Lord, to us belongeth confusion of face, to our kings, to our princes, and to our fathers, because we have sinned against thee.... We have sinned, and have committed iniquity, and have done wickedly, and have rebelled, even by departing from thy precepts and from thy judgments: Neither have we hearkened unto thy servants the prophets, which spake in thy name to our kings, our princes, and our fathers, and to all the people of the land"** (Daniel 9:5-10).

Daniel repeatedly used the words *we, us, our.* He was saying, in essence: "Every one of us is affected!"

The key to it all is found in this verse: **"And whiles I was speaking, and praying, and confessing my sin and the sin of my people Israel, and presenting my supplication before the Lord my God for the holy mountain of my God"** (Daniel 9:20). Daniel said, "Oh God, deal with me while You're dealing with Your people. If there is any iniquity in my heart, bring it out. Show it to me!"

Beloved, the Lord brought this message home to me in the last few weeks. Word came to me that a very slanderous thing had been said about me. It cut me to the heart, wounding me deeply. I cried for a whole week, asking God, "Why me, Lord?"

The next week I was with a friend, and I began to talk about the slander. I named the person who had slandered me and recounted every evil thing this individual had said. I complained, "It's all a lie from the pit of hell—and I'm hurting!"

That night at home, God's Spirit spoke to me: "How is what you did with your friend any different from what was done to you?" I thought, "What are You saying, Lord?" The Spirit whispered, "You slandered that individual in return, by telling what was done to you. You are just as guilty!"

Everything that had been said to me in private, I had repeated and planted in someone else! Immediately, I fell before the Lord in repentance. And ever since, He has been showing me just how careful I have to be with my words.

Not long before that incident, I had received a call from a pastor in the Midwest. The pastor mentioned a certain evangelist who is a mutual acquaintance of ours. He said, "I have to tell you, Brother David, I'm concerned for this man. He needs prayer, and I'm calling to enlist you to pray. He has totally lost his anointing. And every time I see him, he has lost weight. It's all because he's listening to a woman in our town who has a Jezebel spirit. He's under her spell!"

Suddenly, it dawned on me. This pastor meant well and was truly concerned. But he was slandering our evangelist friend—and I was just as guilty for listening to it all!

The Holy Spirit struck my heart while we were still on the phone. I quickly said to the pastor, "Brother, drop it—don't say another word! Leave it in God's hands." I did not want to pollute my lips or poison my spirit. And I believe if I were to talk to the slandered evangelist today, he would say, "Yes, I know those rumors are circulating, and it hurts me. But, no, this woman is not a witch. She's a godly, praying Christian!"

The awful things I had heard about that man had to be dealt with in my own heart. A seed of distrust had been planted in me, and I still feel the hurt from it. Now the only way for that seed to come out is if I pray for my evangelist friend and love him. Only then will all the garbage be uprooted!

A man in our church approached me recently after a worship service. He said he had been bad-mouthing his former church to people in our congregation. But God convicted him about his slander, and now he was miserable over it. The trouble was, he had just received a call from a man in his former congregation who, even though he still attended the church, wanted to gossip about it. The man told me, "I know when he comes to my house, he's going to want to talk about our old church. But I don't want to hear any more gossip. I'm sick of it!"

Evil seeds of slander bring only hurt—both to the planter and to the listener!

Now I Come to the Marvelous Benefits of Repentance!

The book of Daniel mentions several benefits for those who have a repentant heart. Indeed, for all who acknowledge their sin, God does the miraculous!

I want to show you just four of the many benefits of repentance. These four things came to Daniel as the result of his heartfelt confession. And each is available to us if we will repent:

1. One benefit is a new and clearer vision of Jesus Christ.

Read what happened after Daniel's repentance: **"Then I lifted up mine eyes, and looked, and behold a certain man clothed in linen, whose loins were girded with fine gold of Uphaz: His body also was like the beryl, and his face as the appearance of lightning, and his eyes as lamps of fire, and his arms and his feet like in colour to polished brass, and the voice of his words like the voice of a multitude. And I Daniel alone saw the vision..."** (Daniel 10:5-7).

Who do you think this person was that Daniel saw in the vision? It was Jesus! What a wonderful benefit the Holy Ghost opened to Daniel when he confessed his sin. He gave him a clear vision of Christ in all His glory!

Please understand: Daniel was not praying for this vision. All he was doing was repenting—confessing and mourning over sin. Jesus took it upon Himself to come to Daniel in this revelation; the Lord initiated it! You see, when we repent and make all things right with God and others, we don't have to seek a revelation. Jesus will manifest Himself to us!

Now, Daniel had friends who were godly also, because he walked only among the righteous. Yet Scripture tells us none of them saw the vision Daniel received: **"...the men that were with me saw not the vision; but a great quaking fell upon them, so that they fled to hide themselves. Therefore I was left alone..."** (Daniel 10: 7-8).

A truly repentant heart never has to hide from the Lord—because there is no longer any fear of judgment! If you acknowledge your sins, evidencing godly sorrow and making restitution, you can look confidently into the Master's face. You don't have to quake with fear when you hear the thundering word of reproof—because you'll see Christ in His glory. You'll stand before His flaming eyes while everyone else is fleeing!

2. A second benefit of repentance is the removal of all fear.

"And, behold, a hand touched me... And he said unto me, O Daniel, a man greatly beloved,

understand the words that I speak unto thee, and stand upright... Then he said unto me, Fear not, Daniel: for from the first day that thou didst set thine heart to understand, and to chasten thyself before thy God, thy words were heard, and I am come for thy words" (Daniel 10:10-12).

Show me a Christian who refuses to acknowledge his sin—who says, "My hands are clean"—and I'll show you someone with a false piety. Such a person puts on a big smile, has a confident walk and boasts that all is well. But it's all a facade! The Bible makes it clear that if anyone hides his sin, that person will not prosper. God lifts His Spirit from him, and his soul is tossed like the waves. His unrepentant heart is full of fear and restlessness!

But show me a repentant Christian—one who is sensitive to sin, willing to be searched, crying out, "I'm guilty, O God!"—and I'll show you one who soon will walk each day without any trace of fear. God will reach His mighty hand into that believer's heart and pluck out all roots of fear. And soon that person will know the immeasurable favor and blessing of God!

"...O Daniel, a man greatly beloved...stand upright..." (Daniel 10:11). Jesus told Daniel, "Stand upright, repentant one! I'm going to take away all your fear and trembling. And I'm going to put you on your feet and bless you with My favor!"

Beloved, let God search and examine your heart. Ask the Holy Spirit to reveal everything you have said or done that is grievous to Him. Think of anyone you have slandered or gossiped about, and admit how sinful it was. Go to that person, or get on the phone, and make restitution.

Now, it's not enough to say, "If I've wronged you in any way..." That isn't repentance. Repentance is admitting that what you did was a sin! So spill it out. Tell the person exactly what you said or did, and then make it right.

I promise you—if you make all things right, you will release in your life such favor from God as you have never known! The Lord will open your eyes, ears and understanding—and you will be given a revelation of things to come: "...(you will) understand what shall befall thy people in the latter days..." (Daniel 10:14).

3. A third benefit of repentance is a new pair of lips.

Daniel was given new lips that had been touched by God's purging hand: **"And, behold, one like the similitude of the sons of men touched my lips: then I opened my mouth, and spake..."** (Daniel 10:16). Now whenever Daniel spoke, he spoke "as unto the Lord"!

Isaiah was a godly man who had issued mighty prophecies. But when he stood before the Lord in all His holiness, this prophet could only say, **"...I am a man of unclean lips..."** (Isaiah 6:5).

God took coals of fire from the altar, put the tongs on Isaiah's lips, and burned out all dross, self and flesh—everything that was unlike Himself. And He gave Isaiah a new pair of lips! I believe the prophet never again had to have his lips purged.

Yet God does this for every person who repents! Once your tongue and lips are purged, you will never again want to speak anything that is unlike Jesus. The words that flow from you will be pure!

4. Finally, a fourth benefit of repentance is peace and strength.

"...peace be unto thee, be strong, yea, be strong. And when he had spoken unto me, I was strengthened, and said, Let my lord speak; for thou hast strengthened me" (Daniel 10:19).

Daniel's soul was in agony. He had been mourning for sin—praying, fasting, weeping—and it left him flat on his face, totally drained. He moaned: **"...my sorrows are turned upon me, and I have retained no strength"** (Daniel 10:16).

Then Jesus came to him and touched his body. And suddenly Daniel was flooded with peace and strength. **"...O man greatly beloved, fear not: peace be unto thee, be strong, yea, be strong...."** (Daniel 10:19). Jesus told Daniel, "O Daniel, I love you. And I want to give you My peace. Now, stand up and be strong!"

The repentant Christian can be downcast, totally wiped out, overwhelmed by sorrow and weariness. But the Lord always comes to touch his body—to give renewed peace and strength!

I ask you: Do you have a repentant heart? Do you want one? Fall on your knees today and cry out in confession—for yourself, your family, your loved ones, your church. You will receive an incredible revelation of the Lord. You'll begin to speak from pure lips. You'll no longer live in fear of any kind. And you will know peace and strength from God's mighty hand.

Best of all, each of these marvelous benefits will be "loaded" upon you daily: **"Blessed be the Lord, who daily loadeth us with benefits, even the God of our salvation"** (Psalm 68:19).

That is when you will know the joy of walking in repentance. **Hallelujah!**

—David Wilkerson was the founding pastor of Times Square Church in New York City. There he ministered to gang members and drug addicts. In 1971, he founded World Challenge, Inc., which supports missionaries and outreaches throughout the world. He died in 2011.

Reprinted by permission: World Challenge, Inc., PO Box 260, Lindale, TX 75771. http://worldchallenge.org

IS GOD OPPOSING THE CHURCH?

by Francis Frangipane

When I speak at citywide prayer conferences, I am often asked to unmask the "spiritual power" opposing the body of Christ in the immediate region. I have even been asked to reveal the "ancient name" of the spirit resisting growth and revival in the churches in the area.

"Do you really want to know the name of the most powerful spirit resisting the majority of Christians?" I ask. Eager faces light up with affirmation.

"It's Yahweh."

My questioners, who suddenly look like a tree full of owls, are always bewildered by my answer. They are sure I misunderstood their inquiry until I explain that according to the Scriptures God Himself "resists the proud" (James 4:6).

God will not excuse pride, especially religious pride. And it is this religious characteristic of it—by which we are boastful of our achievements, puffed up with our knowledge or judgmental toward others—that has the living God standing against many of our efforts to win our cities.

Indeed, religious pride is the worst idolatry, for it seats mankind in the place of God. Jesus said of Himself, "I do not seek My glory; there is One who seeks and judges" (John 8:50).

Every time we seek to exalt ourselves, we come face-to-face with God, who not only seeks glory but also judges those who are self-exalting. Our American tradition of self-promotion, though highly esteemed among ambitious men, is "detestable in the sight of God" (Luke 16:15).

The Old Testament is replete with illustrations documenting God's opposition to man's pride. Time after time, it was not Israel's enemies who thwarted national prosperity; it was God. The Lord allowed Israel's adversaries to humble His people, driving them toward humility, repentance and revival.

God's cry to Israel is also for us today: "Oh, that My people would listen to Me, that Israel would walk in My ways! I would quickly subdue their enemies, and turn My hand against their adversaries" (Ps. 81:13-14).

Yes, terrible powers of darkness have invaded our land. The adversary stalks our streets seeking whom he may devour (see 1 Pet. 5:8). Our hope, however, is not in confronting the enemy; it is in our full surrender to God.

If we truly would "learn of Him," then we, like Jesus, would be "meek and lowly of heart" (Matt. 11:29). And God, who gives grace to the humble, would rescue us from our national decline (see James 4:6).

The promise of the Lord is familiar to us. He says, "If My people, who are called by My name, humble themselves and pray and seek My face, and turn from their evil ways, I will hear from heaven and heal their land" (2 Chr. 7:14).

January 1995, Charisma

Perhaps some of us would say, "I *am* humbling myself and praying." Our humility before God is not complete, however, until we learn to humble ourselves not only before God but before *one another*.

The fact is, because of pride, we have yet to accept what the Lord means by His words, "If My people." We still interpret "My people" to mean *our people*—our limited circle of friends, relatives and Christians whose culture and system of worship is, more or less, like our own.

When the Lord thinks of His people, however, He sees a more expansive group. He sees all those in the city-wide church "who are called by [His] Name." In God's eyes, His people are a diverse group from many denominational and ethnic backgrounds, each of whom has been given distinct gifts and strengths to benefit the entire body of Christ in that city.

We in the church have merchandized our differences and felt threatened by each other's strengths. Exploiting our fears, Satan not only has divided us from others, he has made us proud that we are separate. And it is here in the rending of our relationships that the wounds of our society go unreconciled.

In this, the first-century religious group we most resemble is not the Christians, but the Pharisees, whose name means "the separate."

We want God to heal our land. But the land He intends to heal is that which exists beneath the feet of the unreconciled. Healing will begin to flow only as we become "His people" in our own cities—as we humble ourselves and recognize where each of us has personally failed to reveal Jesus in our relationships with others.

God's remedy for society calls for Christians who are unreconciled to each other to "humble themselves and pray." When white Christians humble themselves and ask for forgiveness from black and Native American believers, God begins to heal their land. When churches of different expressions humble themselves and seek God's face together, a wellspring of life rises from within that new beginning.

Forgiveness washes our culture of yesterday's debris. It is as our knees bend in humility and we ask for forgiveness for our part in the wound between ourselves and others that God hears from heaven—and heals the land beneath our feet.

—Francis Frangipane is the founding pastor of River of Life Ministries in Cedar Rapids, Iowa. He has since retired from his pastoral duties. Before retiring he opened an international online school called In Christ's Image Training (ICIT).

Reprinted by permission *Charisma Magazine* and Strang Communications Company.

January 1995, Charisma

LESSON 9

THE ROBE, THE CROWN AND THE CROSS — STAGES FIVE AND SIX

MAIN PRINCIPLE

Just as Jesus was stripped of His clothes and His dignity, so we need to be stripped of any idols we have. As God reveals them, we must completely tear down all idols in our lives. Then we can enter into God's presence with hearts free of idolatry.

HOW TO DONATE TO ZOE MINISTRIES

Help us deliver the message of Life throughout the World!

In addition to providing support for ZOE missions, curriculum development/translation and course scholarships, many of our translated materials will be donated to believers without resources to purchase them.

Would you prayerfully consider supporting this ministry?

YOU ARE ABLE TO MAKE A DONATION IN ANY OF THE FOLLOWING WAYS:

Online with PayPal Account or Credit Card via PayPal
This gives you a safe and easy way to make designated contributions.

Visit our website to make a secure online donation.
www.zoeministries.org

By Automatic Bill Pay
Recurring donations to ZOE or to a designated ZOE missionary may be set up with your bank.

By Check
Please make checks payable to 'ZOE Ministries International'
Please don't write a missionary's name on the check. Instead include a separate note.
Our Address is – ZOE Ministries International, PO Box 2207, Arvada CO 80001-2207, USA

May God bless you richly for your support of this ministry!

"Now this is eternal life [zoe]: that they may know you, the only true God, and Jesus Christ, whom you have sent." - John 17:3

THE CALLING OF SEPARATION

by Dennis Lindsay

Eight stepping stones for building character are listed in II Peter 1:5-7: "But also for this very reason, giving all diligence, add to your faith virtue, to virtue knowledge, to knowledge self-control, to self-control perseverance, to perseverance godliness, to godliness brotherly kindness, and to brotherly kindness love."

In our walk with the Lord we want to saturate our lives with the knowledge of the Word of God and with things which will reap great dividends. The problem is, we often overlook the second step—virtue, or the calling of separation.

Each of these steps is a calling. The first one—faith, is the calling of salvation. Knowledge is the calling of saturation—saturating our lives with God's Word. Then comes self-control, the calling of service, where we learn to hold our passions in check so that we can better serve one another. Perseverance, or endurance, is the calling of suffering. Some of the difficulties we experience are for our own good. The calling of self-love is goodness—developing a positive outlook toward what God intends from our own life. Then brotherly kindness—the calling of sensitivity to other people's needs. And love—the calling of spiritual re-production.

I would like to focus in on virtue—the calling of separation. We probably don't have a problem with the calling of faith. We can see spiritual evidence in our lives as we grow in the Lord. A new sensitivity to right and wrong results in an increase of testing within our lives, a new love for Christians, and a desire to share what we have with others. These are all evidences of our faith. Although there may be some ways the Lord can speed up the process of spiritual maturity, there are no shortcuts. In Scripture, the Lord demonstrates this through the analogy of unclean versus clean animals in the Levitical laws. Two things clearly determine a clean animal: it chews the cud and it has split hooves. Some animals chew the cud but don't have a cloven hoof. Others have a cloven hoof but do not chew the cud. These are unclean animals.

In the spiritual realm, the split hoof symbolizes the way in which we are to walk: We are to separate ourselves from the ways of the world. There are Christians who love to meditate on the Word, but really don't separate themselves from the ways of the world. Then there are others who are so legalistic that they keep all the laws, but really don't "chew the cud"—allow the Holy Spirit to develop greater flexibility in their relationships with others. The Holy Spirit wants to purify our motives, our real character. We need to identify our motives to see who is really sitting on the throne of our heart.

In his book *Looking Out For Number One*, Robert Ringer says that many people "don't do something for the reason that it's the right thing to do if there's no benefit to be derived from it." Often the values of the world are the reverse of the values God exalts in His Word. Luke 14:12-14 gives us Jesus' perspective: "Then He also said to him who invited Him, 'When you give a dinner or a supper, do not ask your friends, your brothers, your relatives, nor your rich neighbors, lest they also invite you back, and you be repaid. But when you give a feast, invite the poor, the maimed, the lame, the blind. And you will be blessed, because they cannot repay you; for you shall be repaid at the resurrection of the just.' " If you want to be blessed from God's perspective, invite people who will never be able to return anything to you. Matthew 6 says, "Take heed that you do not do your charitable deeds before men, to be seen by them. Otherwise you have no reward from your Father in heaven. …But when you do a charitable deed, do not let your left hand know what your right hand is doing, that your charitable deed may be in secret; and your Father who sees in secret will Himself reward you openly" (Matthew 6:1, 3, 4).

What is virtuous love? We don't really have a good understanding because we shade the truth for our own personal advantage, expressing attitudes, emotions and convictions that are really not our own. To make a good impression, we use words we don't understand, or we claim knowledge we don't have. We acquire things to advertise a status that's beyond us, and we even drop names. To create an image of influence and strengthen our own ego, we say nice things we really don't mean; we cultivate friends we only hope to use; we take credit where it's not due and avoid the blame where it is. And so we build a showcase side to our lives. We learn to present different faces to the world. "The heart is deceitful above all things, and desperately wicked; who can know it?" (Jer. 17:9). If the Lord would expose our spiritual hearts, we would see that often the true reason we do good things is for personal gain.

The book *The Kingdom of Self* by Earl Jabay describes this attitude quite well. "The first thing a baby does when he comes into the world is to establish his kingdom. He of course is a king. He is number one. Because there is none higher than himself, he is in the position of a god. Babies do all of this the first day they're among us. Shortly after birth, the baby is hungry. He is exhausted by a humiliating eviction from quarters which quite frankly he thoroughly enjoyed. Besides his source of food is cut off. A complaint must be registered immediately. The baby cries. He wants service. The weary mom hears, understands and responds, for nothing in all the world is more precious than her baby. …But now our little friend has a new problem. There is an uncomfortable feeling around his buttocks. And because his skin is very tender, he again lets out a cry. Mother quickly responds. She changes the diaper, caresses her beautiful baby and lovingly places him back in the bassinet. Each time the king cries out, he's obeyed. …Each day he tests the au-

thority of his kingdom and each time he is gratified with the results. All he has to do is cry and someone will come running to attend his need. Obviously he is the center of the world. The world exists for him. He is a god. …Every parent can testify to the unbelievable strength and persistence of a young child's will. And that doesn't mention, that doesn't even take into consideration a strong-willed child. The tragedy is, of course, when the child wins the contest of wills, guess what? He loses. Everyone loses. When the will of a child predominates, the result is a spoiled child."

A spoiled child leads to spiritual depravity. The child learns that it's easier to do wrong than right. When he finally comes to the Lord and wants to do what's right, a great struggle begins with the kingdom of self.

Sometimes we choose a vocation as a vacation. Even a calling of the Lord can be based on monetary reasons.

Salvation is not based on easy believism. In fact, the problem is that the altar call often makes discipleship optional. We accept Jesus as Savior, but we don't make Him Lord.

Lordship is mentioned over 700 times in the New Testament, while *savior* is only mentioned 24 times (only twice in the book of Acts). There is a man-centered gospel which feeds the ego and broadens our kingdom. Man accepts Jesus on his own terms, receiving incentives such as escaping hell.

There are principles in the Scripture such as "give, and it will be given back to you." But so often we're tainted with the ways of the world from the day we're born. When we finally accept Jesus as Lord, He wants to clean up our lives, but we're a little reluctant to allow Him to do so. The Gospel of Jesus, on the other hand, is God-centered. It will destroy the ego and the kingdom of self. In the parable about the kingdom of God, Jesus told about the merchant looking for a fine pearl of great worth. Jesus is the great pearl. That Great Pearl has everything for us: joy, peace, healing, security, eternity. So we invite Jesus into our heart. We say, "How much does that cost?" The seller says, "Well, it's very expensive. It costs everything you have: your wife, children, house, garage, cars, money, clothing, job, time—and yourself, too! Now you can *use* all these things, but don't forget, they're mine. And when I need any of them, you must give them to me, because I'm the new owner."

Jesus gives us a blank check, but He also gives us a contract with nothing except a dotted line. We sign it and He fills in the details later.

Finally, when we come to the Lord, we do not accept an invitation. An invitation gives the privilege of acceptance or rejection. But if it's an invitation, why are there consequences and punishment that go along with it? It really is a command.

Look at the examples in Scripture. First is Zacchaeus. In Luke 19:1-10, Zacchaeus knew that Jesus was Lord, and He had come for him. And so he announced, "Lord, I'll give half of my goods to the poor. I'll restore four-fold to all of those I have cheated." And Jesus said, "Salvation today has come to your house" (Lk. 19:8, 9 paraphrased). Jesus didn't explain the plan of salvation or the four spiritual laws. He didn't take him down the Roman Road. All He said was, "Today salvation has come to your house." When did it come? When Zacchaeus obeyed. It wasn't acceptance of a philosophy; it was obedience.

The same thing is true with Matthew, the tax collector. Jesus didn't give Matthew a choice. He simply said, "Follow Me." In other words, this is more than just an invitation. It's a command. If it were an invitation, we would have the right to accept or reject it and still be saved.

The same is also true with the rich young ruler. He asks, "What must I do to be saved?" When Jesus refers to the moral law, he replies, "I've done all those things since I was a child." So Jesus gives him a command. "Go sell all you have, give to the poor and come follow Me" (Matt. 19:16-21 paraphrased). He can't live up to the command, so he goes away sad and unsaved.

The calling of separation supplements your faith with virtue or goodness. Let's identify those things in our lives that will eventually influence us to choose the ways of the world and relinquish them to follow the will of the Lord. Obedience is not an option—it's a command. It's not *a* choice—it's the *only* choice.

—Dennis Lindsay is the President and CEO of Christ for the Nations, which was founded in 1970 by his parents, the late Gordon and Freda Lindsay. Dr. Lindsay has written many books on Creation Science, and teaches that subject at Christ for the Nations Institute in Dallas, Texas.

Reprinted by permission: Christ for the Nations
CFNI, P.O. Box 769000, Dallas, TX 75376-9000,
800-933-2364

ASSIGNED ARTICLE

LEARNING HUMILITY FROM JESUS

by Rick Hufton

"Come to me, all you who are weary and burdened, and I will give you rest. Take my yoke upon you and learn from me, for I am gentle and humble in heart, and you will find rest for your souls. For my yoke is easy and my burden is light." (Mat. 11:28-30)

Jesus makes a most startling statement to us. "*I am gentle (meek) and humble in heart...*" It is startling because of the identity of the One who speaks. Jesus is "*...the image of the invisible God, the firstborn over all creation. For by him all things were created: things in heaven and on earth, visible and invisible.*" (Col. 1:15, 16). Jesus not only created everything, He upholds all things with the word of His power. This is the person who says to us, "Learn humility from Me!"

What kind of humility can we learn from the Creator of all things? What does this say about what humility is at its root? It shows us that humility is not primarily a matter of acknowledging sin, for Jesus had none. Nor can it be essentially acknowledging one's finiteness before an infinite Creator, for it is the Creator who addresses it.

Make no mistake. We must indeed humble ourselves and acknowledge our sins to God in repentance; and we must live with the constant awareness that God made us, not we ourselves. Our physical, mental and spiritual lives are derived from Him. But behind these expressions of humility there lies the root idea of what humility is all about. And it is a truth that we see expressed and demonstrated by the Lord Jesus Himself.

TOTAL DEPENDANCE ON THE FATHER

Jesus' humility was one of complete dependence on God the Father. He did nothing by His own initiative. He lived a life dependent upon and completely yielded to His Father in heaven. Jesus said, "*I tell you the truth, the Son can do nothing by himself; he can do only what he sees his Father doing*" and "*I do nothing on my own but (I) speak just what the Father has taught me.*" (John 5:19; 8:28).

This was the life Adam and Eve were supposed to live in the garden of Eden, and it is the kind of life for which God created all of us. But our first ancestors chose to live life their own way. They yielded to the tempter's lure of god-likeness without God. "You can be just like God all by yourselves. You can do it on your own." This, in essence, was the lie Satan told them and which they believed. And it has been the root of man's spiritual crisis ever since.

Jesus came as a man, to live the life of dependence, of faith and obedience that Adam failed to live. It is the kind of life man was designed to live. We were not made to live independently of our Creator. On the contrary, the need for God was woven into the very fabric of our being. Man on his own, without God, is a weary and burdened creature, struggling to fill the void left by his rejection of God's sovereignty over him.

THE BURDEN OF PRIDE

Jesus appeals to those "who are weary and burdened," because that is the state of those who do not yield their lives to God. The burden of pride is heavy. The price for our independence is a life of toil and struggle, a toil that in the end is fruitless.

Isaiah speaks eloquently to this very issue, as he decries the idolatry of Babylon.

"Bel bows down, Nebo stoops low; their idols are borne by beasts of burden. The images that are carried about are burdensome, a burden for the weary. They stoop and bow down together; unable to rescue the burden, they themselves go off into captivity. Listen to me, O house of Jacob, all you who remain of the house of Israel, you whom I have upheld since you were conceived, and have carried since your birth. Even to your old age and gray hairs I am he, I am he who will sustain you. I have made you and I will carry you; I will sustain you and I will rescue you." (Isa. 46:1-4).

Bel and Nebo were the principle gods of Babylon. Every year, the Babylonians performed a solemn ritual, in which the images of Bel and Nebo were carried about the city in order to bring divine blessing on the nation. They were large images, and no doubt were a great burden to the men who bore them. Isaiah picks up this theme, and declares that their gods are only a burden, nothing more.

Idolatry of any kind represents man's attempt to have a "God" of his own making. Not a God who is holy, and makes demands upon us, but a god with whom we are "free" to pursue our own designs and intentions. But this "freedom" exacts a heavy toll. "The images that are carried about are burdensome, a burden for the weary." It goes against the way God made us, and imposes upon us a burden we were never designed to bear.

In many ways, we are like the little boy who is determined he can do a task on his own. He refuses assistance from his mother with the confident assertion, "I can do it myself!" It takes only a few minutes for him to realize he has bitten off more than he can chew. If the task the boy undertakes is washing the car, we may merely chuckle. But if the lad shows the same bravado about using a chain saw, we would be horrified.

When Adam and Eve went their own way, they "bit off more than they could chew." The human race has been burdened with the same issue ever since. We were not made to be independent, but to be totally dependant on God.

Humility is our recognition of and submission to our dependence on God. Pride is our rejection of this reality, and an attempt to replace God's authority in our lives with autonomy. When we humble ourselves before God, by accepting His rule in our lives, we are freed from that burden. Jesus told us to learn meekness and humility from Him, so He could liberate us from the weary burden of "self rule."

This is the very message that Isaiah brought to God's people. *"…you whom I have upheld since you were conceived, and have carried since your birth. Even to your old age and gray hairs I am he, I am he who will sustain you. I have made you and I will carry you; I will sustain you and I will rescue you."* Notice the contrast between Babylon and us. Babylon makes her own gods; our God carries us. Babylon cannot sustain the burden of her gods (i.e. of self rule); God sustains us.

EASY YOKE, LIGHT BURDEN

How foolish it is of mankind to think they can live without yielding to the One who created them. What a hard lot is theirs. In compassion Jesus cries out, "Come to me, all you who are weary and burdened, and I will give you rest."

It may not seem so at first, but the "freedom" of our own way is a burden we cannot bear. Like the Babylonians, we will grow weary under its weight. We weren't made to carry God; He made us and He carries us and He sustains us!

By contrast to the heavy load of self-rule, Jesus' yoke is easy, and His burden light. It may involve saying "No" to the flesh. It may require leaving behind actions and attitudes, which are familiar and seem to fit well. But, it is an easier yoke than the burden of self-determination.

Jesus understood this, and lived it. He calls on us to learn this lesson of humility from Him, to take His yoke of submission to God's authority.

— Rick Hufton is the senior pastor of Faith Family Church in Fairview Heights, Illinois. He was born of missionary parents but raised in the United States. He was formerly on staff at Grace Church in St. Louis where he was a teacher, worship leader and writer.

Reprinted by permission: Psalmist Magazine

LESSON 10

CARRYING THE CROSS—
STAGES SEVEN AND EIGHT

MAIN PRINCIPLE

Jesus suffered greatly when He was crucified. We need to respond to Jesus' suffering at His crucifixion by choosing to take up our cross and follow Him. We must not be like the Pharisees, who were more concerned with religion than following Jesus.

JESUS CHRIST IS GREAT!

by Paul Lowenberg

Here is the message you and I must take to the nations of the world: Jesus Christ is great! Let Him be great in your life, great in your home, great in your marriage and great in your vision.

G = God

Jesus Christ is great, first of all, because He is God. In the Gospels God meets you in the person of Jesus Christ. Paul said in I Timothy 3:16, "And without controversy great is the mystery of godliness: God was manifest in the flesh…."

God came to the manger—God in diapers, if you will. He came down to become fully and totally human, touched with the feeling of our infirmities. The Father of Eternity became a child of time. The Creator became a creature on this earth.

Who can explain the depths of the mystery of Jesus Christ? At His touch, blind eyes see, dumb tongues speak, deaf ears hear, withered hands raise in prayer and worship, the lame walk, the lepers are cleansed and the demon-possessed are delivered.

He took a little boy's lunch and fed 5,000. He spoke to the wind and the waves and they obeyed Him. He spoke into a tomb, and out came Lazarus—resurrected by the power of God.

On the cross, Jesus reached up with one hand until it laid hold of the hand of His Father. With the other hand, He reached down to a sinking, sinning, dying world. In that last moment of His life, Jesus Christ slipped the hand of sinning man into the hand of a saving God. He clutched those two hands in His own and cried, "It is finished."

R = Redeemer

In the last few years, you and I have seen one of the greatest demonstrations of the corruptible power of money of all time. We have watched what money does to leading politicians, congressmen, lawyers, courts, businessmen, society and tragically, leaders in the world of religion. Men have sold morals, integrity, virtue and honesty for that thing called money. How desperately men need a Savior.

I think of the little boy who decided to make a boat. He found a special piece of wood and began to carve on it. He carved until he had exactly what he wanted—a masterpiece. He rigged it with masts and equipment. He even carved his own initials on the prow of the boat.

One day, the boy went out with his boat and laid it in the water. Before he realized what had happened, the swift current had pulled his little boat out of sight. The boat was going faster than his little feet could run. He followed it as far as he could, but soon it was gone. He was devastated by his loss.

Some weeks later while walking down the street in his little town, the boy looked in a store window. His heart leaped into his throat—there was his boat! He ran into the store and said, "Mister, Mister, that's my boat. I want it!" The man said, "Wait a minute. That's not your boat." The boy explained, "Yes it is, Sir, yes it is! It's got my initials on it. That's my boat." The man said, "No, Son, that's my boat. A man came in here a little while ago and asked how much I would give him for the boat. I gave him the money, so now it's mine."

When the man saw the agony in the little boy's face he said, "Son, if you'll bring me the amount of money I paid for this boat you can have it." But the little boy didn't have any money. His mother and dad helped the boy think of ways to earn some money. Finally, he scraped up enough money to redeem the boat. When he took his fistful of money to the store and laid it on the counter, the storekeeper gave him his boat. The little boy hugged it to his heart. Standing there on the sidewalk, he was heard to say, "Little boat, I made you. Little boat, I lost you. Little boat, I found you. Little boat, I bought you. Now you're twice mine!"

That's what Jesus Christ says of you and me. "You're twice mine—once by creation and now by redemption." "…Ye were not redeemed with corruptible things as silver or gold…But with the precious blood of Christ" (I Pet. 1:18,19). Jesus is great as a Redeemer.

E = Emmanuel

Emmanuel means "God with us." When you're victorious or when you're losing out, when you're healthy or when you're sick, when you're prospering or on the brink of total poverty, when you have friends or when you're alone—God is with you. When you drive that long, weary road from the cemetery, having laid away the dearest of your life, He is still Emmanuel—God with us.

I don't remember a morning when my wife didn't say to our children as they were leaving for school, "Remember, God is with you." God is with you when you get A's or F's, whether you win first place or come in last, whether you're popular or misunderstood, whether you're the teacher's pet or the teacher's pain in the neck; God is with you. He's Emmanuel.

A = Advocate

"My little children, these things write I unto you, that ye sin not. And if any man sin, we have an advocate with the Father, Jesus Christ the righteous" (I Jn. 2:1). This is a message that needs to be preached: Don't play with sin, don't fool around with it, don't parley with it, don't negotiate with it; don't sin!

Paul says to flee immorality, flee youthful lusts, flee idolatry and flee adultery. Too many people are running toward sin instead of away from it—running toward temptation instead of running in the other direction.

This generation has lost its sense of what sin is. Sin has been minimized. But James 1:15 says, "Then when lust hath conceived, it bringeth forth sin: *and sin, when it is finished, bringeth forth death.*" It is said of Moses that he chose to suffer affliction with the people of God rather than to enjoy the pleasures of sin for a season. Sin is a choice. Some say, "Let's play around with a little sex; let's experiment; we have a right." Sin, when it is finished… The song says, "If it feels good, do it." I can show you downtrodden, poor women in the red light district. I can show you men and women with every kind of sexual disease—herpes, syphilis, gonorrhea, and AIDS. Sin, when it is finished… Quit thinking that sin is some little play toy and that you're going to get away with it. You're not. You'll not be the first one to outsmart sin. Treat sin like it's a rattlesnake.

Don't sin. But if you do, remember that you have an advocate—a lawyer, an attorney—in the presence of God pleading for you. His name is Jesus.

T = Triumphant

Jesus Christ is the Triumphant One. My wife sometimes says, "It surely must be hard to be Jesus at Christmastime. Everybody celebrates His birthday, but nobody invites Him." All Americans need is some liquor, a few gifts and Rudolph the Red-Nosed Reindeer. Who needs Jesus?

God is not wanted in government anymore, either. The latest move is to get the chaplain out of Congress. They want to take the name of God off our coins. They don't even want God in the Boy Scouts anymore. The Supreme Court doesn't want God in schools.

My wife and I visited behind the Iron Curtain a few years ago in a place called Bratislava. We were in a little church that perhaps would seat 150. It was full on a Tuesday night. Half the crowd was young people. They were bright, energetic kids. Their clothes revealed that they were poverty stricken, but they were clean, pressed and shiny. Some young people led the song service using an old guitar with strings that had been stretched and stretched until they were tuned in between the cracks. That didn't stop those kids.

They decided to close their part with this: "He is Lord, He is Lord. He is risen from the dead and He is Lord. Every knee shall bow and every tongue confess that Jesus Christ is Lord." In their country, in every block you drove, there was a hammer and sickle fluttering in the wind. Wherever you went, you saw red-coated policemen with submachine guns and mad-looking dogs. There was a rumble and roar of army tanks and men on horses with all their machines. The Secret Service had submachine guns, dogs and all kind of instruments of destruction. And those kids were singing, "Every knee shall bow, every tongue confess that Jesus Christ is Lord." That took guts!

I felt like shouting, "Hear it, Stalin; hear it, Marx; hear it, Gorbachev and your atheistic wife Raisa; hear it, Hitler; hear it, Mussolini; hear it, Mao Tse Tung; hear it, Hirohito; hear it, Saddam Hussein; hear it, Madelyn Murray O'Hare and silly Shirley MacLaine. Hear it: "*Every knee shall bow.*" Every communist knee, every Muslim knee, every Hindu knee, every Shinto knee, every Buddhist knee, every Jewish knee, every occult knee, every New Age knee, every Republican knee and every Democratic knee is going to bow. And every rotten, filthy, deceiving, corrupt tongue is going to confess that Jesus Christ is Lord. Won't that be a day? Jesus Christ is great!

— Paul Lowenberg was an ordained minister for 73 years. In that time he was the superintendent and executive presbyter of the Assemblies of God Church. He also traveled to six continents and planted 20 churches before the Lord called him home.

Reprinted by permission: Christ for the Nations
CFNI, P.O. Box 769000, Dallas, TX 75376-9000, 800-933-2364

HOW TO SEE GOD CLEARLY

by Bob Weis

WE'VE PUT GOD IN A BOX, WHICH PROHIBITS US FROM SEEING HIM CLEARLY.

How do we view God? Every one of us has a different perspective of Who God is, what He can do and how He can do it. Sometimes things in this world cloud our vision of God—things from the past that keep us from seeing what He has for us and what direction He wants us to go.

We can't afford to see God vaguely. To see Him clearly, we need to learn more about Him and about ourselves. That's what submitting our will to God is all about. It's not an easy road; but there's nothing greater than hearing the voice of God and knowing we're doing what He has called us to do.

The prophet Isaiah came into the temple and had a head-on encounter with a holy, living God. The encounter impacted his life, his leadership and thereby the whole nation of Israel. The nation of Judah was supposed to see God, but she didn't. Isaiah's assignment was to go preach to those who *chose* not to listen. "And he (God) said, 'Yes, go. But tell my people this: "Though you hear my words repeatedly, you won't understand them. Though you watch and watch as I perform my miracles, still you won't know what they mean." Dull their understanding, close their ears and shut their eyes. I don't want them to see or to hear or to understand, or to turn to me to heal them" (Isa. 6:9-12 LB).

God is talking about the people He loves. The people of Judah could not see God clearly because of rebellion against God. "Eyes they have, but they do not see; they have ears, but they do not hear" (Psa. 115:5, 6). Rebellion is willful disobedience to the known will of God. It can be summed up in three letters: S-I-N.

In the Old Testament, the people of God went through the same cycle over and over again. First, they became reckless—with their faith, their beliefs and their convictions. They wanted to see how close they could get to the world, not how close they could get to God. Then they began to be ungrateful—taking their relationship with God for granted. Their hearts became hardened and stubborn. This led to rebellion. They willfully disobeyed God, until finally they were spiritually and morally ruined. In the end they were scattered and taken captive by their enemies. In the midst of their ruin, they would repent and turn back to God. Finally restoration came. They would once again be a joyful people of God.

Another mistake God's people made kept them from seeing God clearly: They put God in a box. Basically, they tried to figure out how God worked so they could predetermine how He was going to move.

How does this apply to us today? If one morning God told a person to eat an orange and he ate one, that would be obedience to God. Maybe the second morning God would say the same thing, and he'd be obedient and eat an orange. However, if on the third day the person assumed God wanted him to eat an orange and ate one without His instructing him to do so, he would have put God in a box. What used to be fresh from the Spirit would now be dead legalism.

This kind of response has infiltrated the Church and robbed God's people of a fresh anointing and flow of the Spirit. What's happened? We've put God in a box, which prohibits us from seeing Him clearly.

Third, we can't see God clearly because we have a tendency to see Him through our own temperaments and personalities. In the beginning, God created man in *His* image. But we human beings have a tendency to try to see God in *our* image. We try to understand God in human terms. If we're aggressive, we figure God's aggressive; if we're laid back, we assume God's laid back.

Surely our way must be God's way, which means every other way is wrong. The Apostle Paul talked about this in Romans 12:4-6: "Just as each of us has one body with many members, and these members do not all have the same function, so in Christ we who are many form one body, and each member belongs to all the others. We have different gifts, according to the grace given us" (NIV).

This passage validates who we are in Christ. Each one of us is unique and important. God doesn't want us to be somebody we're not. He wants us to be ourselves; to see God in our own way. But it's important for all of us to come together so we can become the complete body of Christ, gifted and enabled to do what God has called us to do. That gives us balance.

Seeing God through our own eyes causes exclusiveness. When we think our way is the only way, it keeps us from perceiving God properly. We limit what God can do through us because of our perception of Who He is. Let God be God, and you be yourself.

Sometimes we fail to see God clearly because our perception of Him is in direct relationship to how we see our parents. If a person's father was a harsh disciplinarian, then his perception of God the Fa-

ther will probably be the same. If his father was like Santa Claus—giving him everything he wanted—then he might assume God too will give him anything he wants. By looking at God through our own experiences, we fail to see Him clearly.

We also don't see God clearly because of the media. Sad to say, the media has painted a pretty rotten picture of Christianity. That's why our witness is so vital in this earth. You and I are reflective of Who God is. We need to change people's perspective of Him.

We must accept the responsibility of reflecting Jesus Christ to those with whom we come into contact. Everywhere we go, people are looking for an example. In today's world we have a shortage of heroes—of people who are truly living for God. Let's commit ourselves to live in such a way that others may be positively affected, enabling them to see God clearly through us.

Last, we don't see God clearly because of apathy—lack of interest. Many people don't read the Word. How can we see God without reading His Word? If we're too busy to stop and quiet our spirits to hear Him and see Him, we will not know what direction to go.

Isaiah went through a four-fold process before he saw God clearly. We usually experience the same thing. The first step is confusion—chaos or crisis—which causes us to look to God. Isaiah 6:1 says: "In the year that King Uzziah died." King Uzziah was a great king. The people of Judah trusted him and felt secure with him as their king. When he died, they began to lose their sense of security, and they looked for someone to lead them. Isaiah could see God because the throne was empty. The people of Judah recognized their need for God to lead them because their king was gone. Many times we don't look to God until our security is jeopardized.

The next step in the process of seeing God clearly is confession. After Isaiah saw God he said, "Woe to me! … I am ruined! For I am a man of unclean lips, and I live among a people of unclean lips, and my eyes have seen the King, the LORD Almighty" (Isa. 6:5 NIV).

The closer we are to God, the more we will confess who He is, and the more we will see our own unworthiness and confess our sin. Christians don't grow in their walk with the Lord because they don't want to be transparent before God. They know that the closer they get to God, the more they'll have to change.

Seeing God clearly causes us to change. After we confess our sins, God can begin to change us. "Then one of the seraphs flew to me with a live coal in his hand, which he had taken with tongs from the altar. With it he touched my mouth and said, 'See, this has touched your lips; your guilt is taken away and your sin atoned for'" (Isa. 6:6, 7 NIV).

What happened to Isaiah happens to us when we confess our sins. Our guilt is gone and our sins are forgiven. Through Jesus we are free from sin and its guilt. Then God can begin changing us into the likeness of Christ.

With change comes commitment to God. As men and women of God—believers in Christ empowered to do His will—we can't afford to see God vaguely. With the Great Commission to fulfill, we can't allow anything to keep us from seeing God clearly.

The world needs us and the Church needs us—empowered, equipped, trained, submitting to God's will. We need to see God clearly.

—Bob Weis has founded and pastored Christian Life Cathedral and Victory Assembly (formerly called Carrollton Christian Fellowship). He is currently the Senior Pastor of First Assembly in Marble Falls, TX.

Reprinted by permission: Christ for the Nations
CFNI, P.O. Box 769000, Dallas, TX 75376-9000,
800-933-2364

LESSON 11

DEPARTURE FROM HIS PRESENCE— STAGES NINE AND TEN

MAIN PRINCIPLE

We need to understand the significance of Jesus' final words, "It is finished."

It was a shout of victory! Jesus won access to God for us because He was willing to take on our sin and be separated from the Father. As we go into God's presence, we go in humility and gratitude, but also in victory.

WRESTLING WITH GOD

by Jamie Buckingham

One of the modern Greek playwrights wrote of the novice who went to stay on an island with an elderly priest. One afternoon the young cleric, eager to learn, walked with the venerable man along the craggy shore. As their robes swirled in the wind, he finally asked his big question.

"Father, do you still wrestle with the devil?"

"No, my son," the elderly man answered, stroking his white beard. "I have grown old, and the devil has grown old with me. He does not bother me as before. Now I wrestle with God."

"Wrestle with God? Do you hope to win?"

The wrinkled old man looked his young consort in the eye. "Oh no! I hope to lose."

Unfortunately, most of us seldom get to that place in life. We spend our years battling with Satan. The devil, however, is not man's real adversary—God is. God's ways are not our ways. His kingdom is not of this world. His commands run counter to our concepts. Until we are defeated by God, we shall always be miserable.

Last summer, following the diagnosis of cancer in my kidney, I found myself in what I thought was mortal combat with the devil. His voice, so logical and factual, echoed through my mind at night after the house was quiet, striking fear and panic. He would remind me of the doctors' prognosis…chide me for not having bought grave plots…show me the agonized faces of my children and grandchildren peering into my cas-

ket…list, one by one, the sins of my past—and present.

Then I discovered that even minor resistance in the name of Jesus causes him to flee. Of course, he returns—and he did, in the form of another cancer.

Now I am back in the wrestling match. Only this time I am not battling Satan, for I know he is already defeated. Instead, like the old priest, I find myself wrestling with God.

As the radiation treatment gradually shrank the tumor, I had time—a lot of time—to spend on the mat. Our conversations, while gentle, were always pointed.

One quiet afternoon, sitting in the home of my physician in St. Petersburg, Florida, I found myself battling with Jesus' words from Luke 9: "Whoever desires to save his life will lose it, but whoever loses his life for My sake will save it" (v. 24, NKJV).

Did this mean I should not take measures to save my life from the cancer? Surely not, for God had told me to resist evil. No, it meant I was not to save my life for my sake—but so I could be at God's disposal, delighting to do His will.

In that same chapter, Jesus says anyone who does not carry his cross and follow Him cannot be His disciple.

For years I had equated the "cross life" with laying down things that were wrong. Last summer, I spent a month taking moral inventory, purging myself of impurities. This time, however, God wanted more. He was asking me to relinquish the things that were right.

That afternoon, like Jacob at Peniel, I wrestled with God. To give up that which is wrong in the face of death is easy. But to surrender just when you see hope for living?

"Do you mean I must nail *everything* to the cross?"

"You are to count yourself as a dead man." (Those identical words were echoed when a friend called from Arizona the next weekend, saying God had spoken them to his wife for me.)

One by one, the list of things "most precious " scrolled across my mind—much longer than last summer's list of sins. It included not only what I liked to do, but also what He Himself had promised. Dreams. Ambitions. Ministry. Family. Health. Even the things I did for God.

Special remembrances were highlighted: playing basketball with my younger friends, climbing mountains in Israel, walking the beach with my wife. All were to be nailed on the cross—with no promise of return.

It's not done yet. Not that I don't want to relinquish those things. I just don't know how to—and stand firm on the word He's given me. Last night He reminded me not to worry about it, bringing to mind 2 Timothy 2:13: "If we are faithless, He remains faithful." That helps!

This I know: While God may be my adversary, He is not my enemy. I'm like a child, wrestling with his dad—knowing that when He finally pins me to the mat, He will then lean down and, laughing, kiss my face.

—Jamie Buckingham devoted his talents and sacrificed his time to teach and spread the gospel, eventually becoming an internationally renowned author, columnist and conference speaker. He was a friend to nearly every significant Christian leader in the charismatic movement until his death in 1992 at the age of 59.

Reprinted by permission: Ministries Today

GUARD YOUR AFFECTION FOR CHRIST!

by David Wilkerson

In the first three chapters of Revelation, the apostle John has an amazing vision: He sees Jesus walking in the midst of the seven New Testament churches of Asia. Christ's eyes are aflame, and he's wearing priestly clothes. It is clear he has come to judge these churches in righteousness.

Peter writes, **"...judgment must begin at the house of God..."** (1 Peter 4:17). And now, as Jesus appears among the seven churches, he begins to judge them according to both the good and bad he beholds. These judgments appear in Revelation 2 and 3—both red-letter chapters, meaning every word comes directly from Jesus' lips.

Now, these seven churches were actual congregations, in real localities—the churches of Ephesus, Smyrna, Laodicea, and so on. Yet John hears God's voice speaking not only to these particular churches, but to the church universal—indeed, to every believer who looks for Jesus' soon return.

Jesus begins his judgments by listing the many good things about the churches that bless him and he compliments each church on these things. But he also sees several things that grieve him deeply—and he issues a warning to each church.

His first message is to the Christians at Ephesus—a church founded on the godly teaching of the apostle Paul. Jesus' judgment of the Ephesians is, **"...thou hast left thy first love" (Revelation 2:4).**

When Jesus uses the words "first love" here, he isn't speaking of the immature love we experience when we're first saved. Rather, he's talking about exclusive love. He's saying, "I once occupied first place in your heart. But now you've lost the exclusivity of your love for me. You've allowed other things to take my place!"

It is significant that of all the sins Jesus points out in these seven churches—adultery, covetousness, lukewarmness, false teachings, Jezebels in authority, dead worship, spiritual blindness—the first sin he names is the one that grieves him most: a loss of affection for him. Our God is a jealous lover—and he won't allow anything to come before our love for him!

I Believe of All the Seven Churches, the Christians at Ephesus Wounded Christ the Most!

David writes, **"Yea, mine own familiar friend, in whom I trusted, which did eat of my bread, hath lifted up his heel against me"** (Psalm 41:9). I identify with David's words. The people in my life who are able to wound me most easily are those who love me the most. My halfhearted friends can't truly hurt me, nor can my enemies. But those who claim to be closest to my heart can wound me deeply.

Now, these Christians at Ephesus had walked closely with the Lord. As I read through Paul's letter to the Ephesians, I'm amazed at the gospel these people heard and lived. In fact, Paul compliments them at length. He addresses them as **"... the faithful in Christ Jesus...blessed...with all spiritual blessings in heavenly places in Christ...chosen...before the foundation of the world...predestinated...unto the adoption of children by Jesus Christ to himself, according to the good pleasure of his will"** (Ephesians 1:1-5).

Paul adds that they are a forgiven people, having the revelation of the mystery of Christ and being **"...sealed with that holy Spirit of promise"** (verse 13). He further prays they would have **"...the spirit of wisdom and revelation in the knowledge of him: the eyes of your understanding being enlightened; that ye may know...the exceeding greatness of his power to us-ward who believe..."** (verses 17-19).

These Christians had been made alive, **"...quickened...with Christ...(who) hath raised us up together, and made us sit together in heavenly places in Christ Jesus"** (2:5-6). Paul calls them Christ's **"...workmanship, created in Christ Jesus unto good works...(and) are made nigh [near] by the blood of Christ"** (verse 13). He says that by God's grace, they are **"...grow(ing) unto an holy temple in the Lord...through the Spirit"** (verses 21-22).

What a description of a blessed, holy people! And now, in the book of Revelation, Jesus also compliments the Ephesian Christians. He tells them, **"I know thy works, and thy labour, and thy patience..."** (Revelation 2:2). In other words: "I know all the good things going on in your lives. You patiently labor for me without complaining. And you'll do anything for others. You're diligent in your good works—and that is very commendable!"

Jesus continues to compliment them, pointing out **"...how thou canst not bear them which are evil..."** (same verse). He's saying, in essence, "You hate sin with a passion! You don't tolerate it—in your life, your home or your church. You have good moral standards. And that also is commendable!"

"...thou hast tried them which say they are apostles, and are not, and hast found them liars" (same verse). Jesus is saying, "You're rooted and grounded in sound teaching. And so you haven't been tossed about by all the latest teachings of the flesh. You're able to rightly judge false teachers and false prophets. And you expose them as liars, for the benefit of everyone among you. I commend you for this as well!"

"...thou hatest the deeds of the Nicolaitans, which I also hate" (verse 6). In other words: "You reject antinomianism—the doctrine that says simply having faith allows man to do as he pleases. Indeed, you hate all doctrines of easy believism that say God overlooks the deeds of the flesh. You faithfully stand up against unholy lifestyles, and you cling to righteousness. This also is highly commendable!"

It quickly becomes evident in this passage that the Ephesians are not just a bunch of novices or lukewarm saints. No, Jesus is examining the hearts of a people who are well-grounded in the truth of the gospel—and who work to prove it in their lives, by sacrificing, laboring and standing up for truth.

Yet Jesus points out something else in the hearts of these Ephesians as well—something he notes is deeply wrong. He says, "I see all your works—your hatred for sin, your love for truth, your righteous courage. And yet somehow in all your labors, you've allowed your first love to wither. Your affection for me is dying!"

"Nevertheless I have somewhat against thee, because thou hast left thy first love" (verse 4). Beloved, I have read and reread this verse—and I have concluded its seriousness cannot be overlooked. The word "somewhat" here—indicating something that might be taken lightly—does not appear in the original Greek text. Instead, the original phrase is translated, literally, "I have something against you!"

Now, I would like to think I'm an Ephesian-type Christian, someone who's a faithful laborer. I want to believe that my suffering is for Jesus' sake, that my good works glorify him, that I practice righteous living, that I'm seated with him in heavenly places.

But when I read of Jesus walking among such well-taught believers as the Ephesians and telling them, "I have something against you"—it grips my soul! I have to ask my Lord: "Jesus, do you have something against me? Have I also lost my affection for you?"

Christ's Warning Isn't Just for Christians of a Bygone Era—But for Us Today!

I believe this warning to the Ephesians is intended for me personally—as well as for every Christian living in these last days! Simply put, the Lord is telling us, "It's not enough for you to be a caring, giving, diligent servant who grieves over sin and preaches truth. It's not enough for you to uphold moral standards, endure suffering for my sake, or even be burned at the stake for your faith. This is all part of taking up my cross.

"You can do all these things in my name. But if in the process of doing them your affection for me does not increase—if I am not becoming more and more the one great delight of your heart—then you have left your first love! If your affection for me is no longer a matter of great concern to you, then I have something against you!"

Consider David's words: **"Whom have I in heaven but thee? And there is none upon earth that I desire beside thee"** (Psalm 73:25). These are strong words—yet David isn't saying, "I don't have human love." He knows God has blessed human love. Rather, David is saying, "There is no one I love exclusively in my heart as I love my Lord. I desire him above all others!"

David also writes, **"O God...my soul thirsteth for thee, my flesh longeth for thee in a dry and thirsty land, where no water is"** (63:1). **"As the hart [deer] panteth after the water brooks, so panteth my soul after thee, O God. My soul thirsteth for God, for the living God..."** (42:1-2).

David says, "I thirst deeply for the Lord, the way a deer thirsts after it has been chased. A deer will go past the point of exhaustion to find the water it seeks!"

Likewise, Jesus is telling the Ephesian Christians, "You no longer seek me as the deer does. I'm no longer the chief object of your desire. You may be willing to do things for me—but I'm not at the center of your heart anymore!"

Christians Have Lightly Skimmed Over This Passage in Revelation for Years!

Some believers might respond, "What's so serious about this matter? Maybe I'm not as intense for the Lord as I was when I was younger. And maybe I've slacked off in my affection for him. But, so what? Jesus knows I still love him."

No! Jesus takes any lack of affection very seriously. Indeed, he says such a lack constitutes a fall: **"Remember therefore from whence thou art fallen, and repent..."** (Revelation 2:5).

You might answer, "I can understand how an act of adultery is a fall. And I can see how falling back into drugs or alcohol is a fall. But how can losing an intense love for Christ really be a fall?"

When Jesus warns, **"...repent, and do the first works..."** (same verse), he's saying: "Think back to what you were like when I first saved you. You rejoiced that I came to live in your heart! You couldn't wait for church on Sunday, just to tell people how much you loved me. And you spent all your free time digging into my word, learning about my love for you. You never considered prayer a burden, because I meant everything to you. You loved me more than life itself.

"But now you've fallen away from all that. I get so little of your time now, so little of your attention. You've grown cold toward me. Something else has your heart!"

Jesus attaches a serious warning to this verse: **"...repent, and do the first works; or else I will come unto thee quickly, and will remove thy candlestick out of his place, except thou repent"** (same verse). For many years theologians have tried to soften this warning, wanting it to mean something different. But it can't be softened! It means exactly what it says. Jesus is saying to us:

"If you claim to have the fire of God, and yet I am no longer the delight of your heart—I will take away every bit of light you have! No matter what good works you do for me, you will no longer be my witness. I simply won't recognize anything you do—because you've lost your love for me!"

There are several signs and evidences of a dying love for Christ. I want to list three of these for you. I believe you can measure your love for Jesus by examining these three things:

1. Your Love for Christ Is Dying if You Spend More Time on the Things of This World and Less Time in His Presence!

What holds your heart right now? Does your soul yearn for Jesus, or for the things of this world?

Not long ago, I received a distressing letter from a woman on our mailing list. She wrote: "My husband was once on fire for God. For years he gave himself faithfully to the Lord's work. But today he's all wrapped up in his new pursuit—horses! He bought several, and he has become absolutely consumed with them. Now, instead of getting into God's word, he spends all his free time reading about breeding horses. He no longer has any time for the Lord, or for me. I worry for him, because he's grown so cold!"

Of course, there is nothing wrong at all with owning horses or having an interest in them. But Jesus told a parable about this very kind of legitimate pursuit. A wealthy man sent his servant to invite all his friends to a great feast he was holding. But, scripture says, the man's friends **"...all with one consent began to make excuse..."** (Luke 14:18).

One friend told the servant, "I just bought a piece of land sight unseen, and I have to inspect it. Please tell your master I won't be able to come." The next friend told the servant, "I just bought a yoke of oxen, and I haven't had time to test them. Tell your master I can't come, because I have to go into the field to plow with them." Yet another friend told the servant, "I just got married, and I'm about to take my honeymoon. I don't have time to come to the feast."

This man had invited all his friends to enjoy an intimate time of fellowship with him. And he had made all the arrangements for their comfort and convenience. The table had been set, and everything had been prepared. But no one came. Everyone was simply too busy or preoccupied.

Yet each person had a good, legitimate reason for not coming. After all, they weren't avoiding their friend so they could go partying or bar-hopping. On the contrary, the Bible commends everything these people were doing: Buying and selling can provide security for one's family. And testing a major purchase is a sound business practice. Finally, marriage is a blessing that the scriptures encourage.

Yet, how did this wealthy man react? Scripture says, **"The lord said unto the servant, Go out into the highways and hedges, and compel them to come in, that my house may be filled. For I say unto you, that none of those men which were bidden shall taste of my supper"** (verses 23-24).

Jesus is making a very clear point in this parable: Each of these good, legitimate things becomes sinful when it takes priority over the Lord!

Let me give you an example. A favorite after-church activity for many Christians is to go to a restaurant with friends. They're able to sit and talk for hours about the things of God over a sandwich or a cup of coffee. And once they exit the restaurant, they spend another half hour talking in the parking lot before parting. It's a time of wonderful fellowship for everyone. Yet, when asked, many of these same Christians claim they have no time to seek the Lord!

During my early years in ministry, I had several godly friends whom I admired for their devoted prayer lives. They spent hours on their faces in God's presence—and their sermons showed it. They preached with fire, unction, life!

Some of these men later went to seminary, seeking a deeper knowledge of the Bible. They dug deep into Hebrew and Greek studies, trying to know the scriptures better. And their studies demanded they read many outside texts.

In the end, however, many of these men lost their fire for Jesus. Why? They spent so much time reading legitimate things—literature, commentaries, textbooks—they neglected to study God's word for themselves. Their pursuit of knowledge robbed them of their affection for Christ!

Any "good" or "legitimate" thing becomes sinful when it takes priority over the Lord!

2. You Can Measure Your Love for Christ by How Deeply You're Affected by Anything That Robs You of Quality Time Alone With Him.

If you can go about your daily life facing all kinds of interruptions and demands, and yet not spend ten minutes in God's presence—your love is dying!

Think about it: If you love someone exclusively above all others, you'll make that person feel he's the most important being on earth. Everything else will pale in comparison to him.

Isn't this how you first loved your spouse, when you were courting? If she called on the phone while you were busy doing something, you dropped everything just to talk to her. And if anyone intruded on your time alone together, you resented it! Your one desire was to develop the love between you. Everything else took second place.

Yet many Christians today go for weeks, even months, without spending quality time with Jesus. He stays on the backburner at all times. They may testify, "I love Jesus with all my heart"—but how can this be true, when they neglect him for days on end?

In Song of Solomon, the bride could not sleep because her beloved **"...had withdrawn himself..."** (Song of Solomon 5:6). This woman arose in the middle of the night, saying, **"... my soul failed...I sought him, but I could not find him; I called him, but he gave me no answer"** (same verse). So she quickly ran into the streets, looking everywhere for her lover, and crying out, "Have you seen my beloved?"

Why was this such a serious matter to her? It was because, she said, **"...This is my beloved, and this is my friend..."** (verse 16). **"...I am sick of love [faint with desire for him]"** (verse 8). She couldn't be without her beloved!

I know a couple who are having serious marital problems. The husband told me, "My wife has never made me feel I'm important to her. I take second place to everyone else in her life!"

This man has to travel a great deal in his work. Once, when he called his wife from the road, she told him she was planning a romantic dinner for his return. It would be just the two of them, a time of romance and intimacy. For days the husband looked forward to that special evening. And finally, when he walked through the front door, it was just as his wife had promised: She was wearing his favorite dress. And she had prepared his favorite meal.

Ten minutes into dinner, however, the phone rang. The man touched his wife's hand and said, "Let it ring. I've so looked forward to this time with you."

She replied, "No, it could be important," and quick-

ly got up to answer the phone. He pleaded with her, "Please! Let's enjoy our time together just this once." She assured him, "I'll only be a minute."

Half an hour later, she came back and announced, "That was Mother. She's depressed, so I invited her over. She needs to be with people tonight."

This man felt completely cut out of his wife's life. There was always someone else, or some kind of interruption, that seemed more important to her than himself. He told me, "She spends hours talking with her friends or counseling people. Yet every time I ask her for quality time, she says she doesn't have any for me. This can't be love!"

I ask you—how does Jesus feel when he spreads the table, anxiously awaits our company, and yet we never show up? The Bible calls us his bride, his beloved, his one great love; it says we were created for fellowship with him. So, what kind of rejection must he feel when we continually put others before him?

3. Your Love for Christ Is Dying if You Have Given in to a Besetting Sin!

I'm not speaking here of Christians who still wage warfare with their sin—who are not yet free from it and continue to hate it. Such believers faithfully cry out to God, believing the Holy Ghost to empower them to victory over their lustful habits.

No, I'm speaking instead to those who think they can continue being a witness for Christ while giving in to their bosom sin. They've given up the spiritual war with their lust—surrendering to it completely!

I received a sad letter from a pastor recently. His wife had watched as his relationships grew worse and his ministry failed. Finally, as she was cleaning one day, she found a stash of pornographic videos. She confronted her husband with them and threw them out.

But the man later sneaked out to the dumpster and retrieved the videos. He admitted he couldn't let go of them! Now he wrote to me, saying, "Brother Dave, please pray for me. I've left the ministry and am teaching school—but none of my fellow teachers respect me."

Why doesn't this man have any respect? It's because his candlestick has been removed! He couldn't be Christ's witness on the job—because the Lord was no longer with him. No matter how many tears he sheds or confessions he makes, he will remain among the living dead as long as he holds onto his sin.

Yet how different it was when a young man came to me, weeping and confessing, "Pastor Dave, I fell back into sin! I got high and nearly overdosed. But as I stood at the brink of hell, I saw how my sin hurt Jesus. I can't do this to him anymore!" As I prayed with him, he cried out in sorrow, "Lord, I'm so sorry for how I hurt you!"

That young man's candlestick will not be removed. His light will again shine! You see, Jesus promises in this same passage, **"...repent, and do the first works... To him that overcometh will I give to eat of the tree of life, which is in the midst of the paradise of God"** (Revelation 2:5, 7). God promises paradise to all who repent!

Is your love for Jesus exclusive? Do you regularly take quality time to be with him? Or have other things crept into your heart, taking up your thoughts and affections? Jesus is asking you right now to repent and start all over again. He wants you to stop and realize, "Wait a minute—I see how this thing has crept into my life. And it's robbing me of my exclusive love for Jesus! I can't let this go on any longer. I've got to go back to my affection for him. Lord, forgive me! Light my candle anew!"

Go back to your first love today. Ask him for grace and strength to begin again to guard your affection for Christ!

— David Wilkerson was the founding pastor of Times Square Church in New York City. There he ministered to gang members and drug addicts. In 1971, he founded World Challenge, Inc., which supports missionaries and outreaches throughout the world. He died in 2011.

Reprinted by permission: World Challenge, Inc., PO Box 260, Lindale, TX 75771. http://worldchallenge.org

MAKING A HABITATION FOR THE LORD

by David Ravenhill

Building a habitation for the Lord is vital to our spiritual growth. We must create an environment that is conducive to maintaining an ongoing relationship with God. Habitation means: "a dwelling or a house: the natural abode or locality of a plant or an animal; a place where someone or something is usually found."

In Scripture, habitation is translated *tabernacle*—God's dwelling place. It's a residence, a dwelling, a place of rest, a place to abide. The Old Testament tabernacle was the place where God dwelt. It was a place where He could rest, settle, feel comfortable and at home.

Paul writes in Ephesians 2:22 that we "are being built together for a dwelling place of God in the Spirit." Under the new covenant, God's Spirit inhabits every believer. "Then the LORD spoke to Moses, saying: 'Speak to the children of Israel, that they bring Me an offering. From everyone who gives it willingly with his heart you shall take My offering…And let them make Me a sanctuary, that I may dwell among them'" (Ex. 25:1, 2, 8). This is as true today as it was back then. God longs to dwell with His sons and daughters.

God expresses His desires, as well as His demands. "According to all that I show you, that is, the pattern of the tabernacle and the pattern of all its furnishings, just so you shall make it" (Ex. 25:9). Not only does God have a desire to dwell in the midst of His people, but He has certain specifications as to what *sort* of place we are to prepare for Him. God is particular; He will not dwell just anywhere.

A sanctuary is a clean place, a consecrated place, a place set apart. If God is going to dwell in our lives, He demands a sanctuary. The tabernacle in the Old Testament was a miniature copy of God's dwelling place in heaven. Moses was taken up into the mountain where God showed him the plan of the tabernacle—a replica of what God was used to in heaven. The King of kings and the Lord of lords desires—and we should give Him our best.

In the book of Revelation, we are invited into God's house. "After these things, I looked, and behold, a door standing open in heaven…A trumpet speaking with me, saying, 'Come up here.'…Immediately I was in the Spirit; and behold, a throne set in heaven, and One sat on the throne" (Rev. 4:1, 2).

The first thing that John was conscious of as he stepped through the front door of God's habitation was the throne and One sitting on the throne. If God is going to dwell in our lives, He demands to sit on the throne, His natural abode. If we are going to develop an intimacy with God, we have to abandon the throne—which represents the authority of God. We will never progress spiritually until we have settled this issue: *Who is on the throne of my life*? Can we honestly say that we have made Jesus Lord?

Secondly, John is arrested by the fact that there is a continual chorus of holiness to the Lord around the throne. "The four living creatures, each having six wings, were full of eyes around and within. And they do not rest day or night, saying: 'Holy, holy, holy, Lord God Almighty, Who was and is and is to come!'" (Rev. 4:8). It isn't something they do at a certain time. They're not just holy on Sunday between 10:00 a.m.

and noon or when they are with a particular group, but they are holy continually—day and night.

Are we holy day and night? What about when nobody else is around—what things do we watch, listen to, read or participate in? Can we honestly say, day and night, that we live a holy life? If we are going to prepare a habitation for God, it has to be holy.

Several years ago, my wife and I learned about a beautiful vacation spot in New Zealand, located in a valley with mountains on either side and a flowing river. Farmers had bought adjacent farms and rented them out as vacation sites. I thought it would be great to get away for a week. The farmhouse was located in a magnificent area, but as we walked in the house we saw it was an absolute mess. The springs were coming up through the couch, and a filthy, old piece of carpet was on the floor. Bottles lined the wall and the shelves in the kitchen. My first thought was, "How are we going to live here?" I wonder if God ever feels that way when He tries to settle in our dwelling place. Can He rest there? "Be holy, for I am holy" (I Pet. 1:16).

Third, John was conscious that God's dwelling place was a place of thanksgiving. "The living creatures give glory and honor and thanks to Him who sits on the throne, who lives forever and ever" (Rev. 4:9). God likes an atmosphere of gratitude. We are to enter His gates with thanksgiving and His courts with praise (Psa. 100:4). Are we thankful? In the place where God dwells, there is a continual chorus of thanksgiving. If He is going to reside in our lives, He does not want us grumbling, complaining and murmuring all the time.

Fourth, John was aware that God's habitation is a place of worship. "The twenty-four elders fall down before Him who sits on the throne and worship Him" (Rev. 4:10). The first time worship is mentioned in the Word of God, it is associated with Abraham. When God told Abraham to sacrifice his only son, Isaac, Abraham responded without any hesitation whatsoever. Taking Isaac, he said to his servants, "Stay here…the lad and I will go yonder and worship" (Gen. 22:5).

What is worship? Worship is our response to the will and purpose of God, regardless of circumstances or cost. Worship is that response from the heart: "Lord, whatever You ask us to do, regardless of the situation, we will do it. It may not make sense to our reasoning; it may bypass our human understanding; but Lord, if You ask us to do it, we'll do it."

When the Bible says God is looking for those who will worship Him in spirit and truth, it means He's interested in the heart that surrenders to Him. The Father seeks those who have a responsive heart that doesn't question or argue. Like Abraham, we are to arise with the most precious thing we have, and place it on the altar of sacrifice.

Fifth, the throne of God was a place of humility. "The twenty-four elders…cast their crowns before the throne, saying: 'You are worthy, O Lord, to receive glory and honor and power'" (Rev. 4:10, 11). In Scripture, the crown speaks of achievement, reward and attainment. Paul says, "Finally, there is laid up for me the crown of righteousness" (II Tim. 4:8). We take that crown representing achievement and recognition and cast it at His feet. We must say, like John the Baptist, "He must increase, but I must decrease" (Jn. 3:30).

If we're going to produce a habitation suitable for the presence of God, it needs to embody all these things. He must sit on the throne of our life. We must have holiness and purity of heart. We must maintain a constant state of thanksgiving and worship. And we must respond to Him with humility. If we produce the right environment, the presence of God will dwell with us.

— David Ravenhill, the son of Leonard Ravenhill, is an international teacher, author and speaker. He has worked with Teen Challenge, Youth With a Mission, was on the pastoral team of New Life in New Zealand, and was on staff at the International House of Prayer in Kansas City. He also spoke at the Brownsville Revival School of ministry.

Reprinted by permission: Christ for the Nations CFNI, P.O. Box 769000, Dallas, TX 75376-9000, 800-933-2364

LESSON 12

PAST THE VEIL AND INTO HIS PRESENCE

MAIN PRINCIPLE

We can now enter the Holy of Holies, the presence of God the Father. We do this only through the shed blood of Jesus, which cleanses us from sin. We can go into God's presence with confidence through Jesus, our new and living way.

SEVEN WOMEN SHALL LAY HOLD OF ONE MAN!

by David Wilkerson

THE GLORY OF GOD IN HIS CHURCH IN THE LAST DAYS

According to the prophet Isaiah, two kinds of churches will exist in the last days. And I believe these two types of churches are already in existence. We do not have to speculate about what they will be like—because Isaiah gives us a very clear, prophetic description of both.

Isaiah 4 opens with a concise and tragic description of what I call "the church of forgiveness only": **"And in that day seven women shall take hold of one man, saying, We will eat our own bread, and wear our own apparel: only let us be called by thy name, to take away our reproach"** (Isaiah 4:1).

This is one of the most misunderstood verses in all the Bible. Some commentators suggest this happened during the reign of King Ahaz, when enemy armies came in and slew 120,000 men. But that is only speculation. There is no evidence that this verse has ever been fulfilled at any time in history. There is nothing to suggest that, even in Ahaz' time, seven women "took hold of one man."

Then the Holy Spirit spoke something to me concerning this passage. To my knowledge, you won't find what I have to say in any commentary. Yet, I see this entire chapter in Isaiah as one of the clearest, most un-mistakable prophecies about how the church will look just prior to the coming of the Lord.

Like many Christians, I believe without a doubt we are living in the last days. Jesus' life, death and resurrection instituted the beginning of this period. On the day of Pentecost, Peter stood up and said, **"...this is that which was spoken by the prophet Joel; and it shall come to pass that in the last days, saith God, I shall pour out of my Spirit upon all flesh..."** (Acts 2:17). Peter was saying, "These are the last days. God's outpoured Spirit is proof of it!"

Likewise, the apostle Paul wrote, **"Now all these things happened unto them for examples: and they are written for our admonition, upon whom the ends of the world are come"** (1 Corinthians 10:11). Paul knew he was living in the last days. And to me, there is no question that we are living in the very last of the last days!

In Revelation 1, John sees Jesus standing in the midst of seven golden candlesticks: **"...and his eyes were as a flame of fire; and his feet like unto fine brass, as if they burned in a furnace..."** (Revelation 1:14-15).

John was smitten by this frightful sight—and he fell

on his face in fear! Remember, this was the same John who once leaned his head on Jesus' bosom. And now, as he sees the Lord in this state, he is utterly stricken.

Scripture makes it very clear that these seven candlesticks represent seven churches—that is, the entire religious body of believers in the last days, all that we call "the church." And Jesus walks among these seven candlesticks, His piercing eyes searching the seven churches.

Scripture Always Refers to the Church in the Feminine Gender, in Many Cases as a Bride.

The seven would-be brides Isaiah mentions are clearly a type of the characteristics of many in the last-days' church.

Dispensationalists would say the seven churches of Revelation represent seven church ages. I am saying that I believe you will find the characteristics of all seven churches in all churches through the ages. Even in "blessed" churches that are complimented by the Lord—such as are of the spirit of Smyrna or Philadelphia—you will find mixture and characteristics that God hates.

These seven would-be brides are seeking to lay hold of one man, whom I take to be Christ. Yet these brides are not interested in loving Him. On the contrary, they have only one thing on their minds—the removal of their reproach!

"...We will eat our own bread, and wear our own apparel: only let us be called by thy name, to take away our reproach" (verse 1).

I see here seven women approaching a man and saying, "You don't have to provide food for us. We'll take care of our own bread. And you don't have to provide any clothes for us. We'll provide our own robes."

You don't have to be very deep spiritually to see the significance here. After all, **"...sin is a reproach to any people"** (Proverbs 14:34)—reproach of guilt! Sure, these women want to be the bride of Christ—but only on their own terms. They want an arrangement without intimacy, love or devotion.

The number seven is used in regard to these brides to remind us that in every church system there are such people. They attempt to "take hold of one man"—Christ—only to get relief from the guilt and condemnation of their sin. They don't want intimacy with Him. They want nothing more than forgiveness—to have the reproach of sin removed. I call this "the church of forgiveness only."

Please understand—I believe in justification by faith. It is by faith alone in Jesus Christ that we are saved. We are justified by His finished work on the Cross. And because of this we can live without guilt, fear or condemnation. This is the great meaning of the gospel.

But if that is all you ever want of Jesus—if you don't want to be intimate with Him, to live on Him as the bread from heaven, and to come under His fiery gaze, which searches and convicts—then being forgiven is your entire focus!

I was in a town some time ago to speak at a meeting, and I passed a big amphitheater advertising a Christian rock concert. I stopped to watch the kids set up their equipment for the show. Unbelievably, some of them wore T-shirts with a message that included a four-letter word. It read: "— Guilt!"

I can't even quote the word to you here—and these were so-called Christians. Apparently, all they wanted was to get rid of guilt!

Many pastors and evangelists today preach a "forgiveness only" message—and that's all they preach! They cry, "Come, accept Jesus and enjoy a life without guilt, fear or condemnation. Just believe and confess, and you will be His bride. You can walk your own walk and talk your own talk!"

I do not believe we are saved by the law—but the law has a purpose. It is a mirror that holds up before us the commands and demands of God. And when we see we can't fulfill those commands, we are driven to Jesus. But God help us if we don't hear this kind of preaching!

Many churches have replaced the Word with ten-minute skits that contain no convicting gospel at all. There is no preaching of holiness, no word of separation from the world, nothing about sanctification or dealing with besetting sins. Yet the leaders defend themselves by saying, "People don't want to hear a hard gospel. We're simply giving them what they need to cope in these troubled times."

Indeed, the Bible says of those who attend such churches, **"...after their own lusts shall they heap to themselves teachers, having itching ears"** (2 Timothy 4:3). These churchgoers are saying, "You don't have to feed us, Jesus. We can provide our own bread. We have our own gospel!"

All across America churches are feeding their sheep the same pabulum—a cotton candy, "feel-good" gospel. These places are packed with thousands who have merely repeated a sinner's prayer, saying, "I believe!" But the Bible says even the demons believe—and they tremble at the very thought of God!

Few of these people have been provoked to deny self and embrace the Cross—to die to all self and ungodliness. They don't want the burden of the Lord. They don't weep over the sins of Zion. They don't feel God's heartbrokenness over the wickedness and compromise in these last days.

Instead, they say, **"...We will eat our own bread..."** (Isaiah 4:1). They don't want the bread that comes down from heaven—that is, Jesus Christ crucified, resurrected and seated at the right hand of the Father. He is the bread of separation—of holiness, purity, self-denial. But these say, "We will provide our own bread"—usually a gospel of permissive love, with no reproof, no smiting conviction.

Beloved, the Bible says their bread is defiled! The prophet Hosea called it **"...the bread of mourners; all that eat thereof shall be polluted: for their bread for their soul shall not come into the house of the Lord"** (Hosea 9:4).

Yet the true house of God—the holy remnant church—will have nothing to do with this manmade bread. They know that most of it is pop psychology, with a few verses of Scripture sprinkled in to make it sound religious. It sounds good—but leaves the sheep starving!

"...We will...wear our own apparel..." (Isaiah 4:1). The "church of forgiveness only" says, "Listen, Lord,

you don't have to provide us with clothes. We'll make our own and clothe ourselves." There are no robes of righteousness for this people—no holiness preaching, no reproof, nothing "negative." There is no separation from the world, no forsaking of all others, no cleaving to their husband. Instead, they say, "We will dress as we please!"

These would-be brides have no desire to submit to the authority of a husband. They don't want to live under the same roof with him. Nor are they interested in his needs. They don't want to know his heart or care about his concerns. They are totally consumed with self—with having their reproach removed!

So they have as little contact with him as possible—maybe one hour a week. Is there any intimacy, love, companionship, submission in this arrangement? No! Is there any clinging to Him? No! Do they desire to spend hours in His presence—in secret, sharing His very heart? No—they spend most of their time with "other loves," such as sports, TV, theater, pleasures of all kinds. Without exception, such Christians always turn to a self-centered gospel.

A man who was visiting our church recently from a large southern city approached me before one of our services. He said, "Brother David, I just had to leave my church. We sent a whole delegation across the country to a congregation where a 'great revival' was supposedly taking place. Everyone came back excited about it all—but something didn't sit right in my spirit. I didn't feel I could be a part of this 'new thing.' So I had to leave.

"Tell me—what is happening to our church? Where is the discernment? Why isn't our pastor intimate with Jesus? Why doesn't anyone seem to know God's heart? Why this sudden introduction of an 'imported' revival?"

Indeed, it is out of intimacy with Jesus that we receive discernment, direction, a knowing of what is right and wrong, of what is holy and pure. Intimacy with Christ gives us a firmness wherein we are not tossed to and fro by every wind and wave of doctrine. Yet right now there is such foolishness going on, with no discernment at all. It is manmade bread—it is not of God—and it grieves His heart!

Now, let me move on to the other church of which Isaiah speaks:

The Next Church Isaiah Saw Emerging in the Last Days Is Called the Church of God's Glory!

"In that day shall the branch of the Lord be beautiful and glorious, and the fruit of the earth shall be excellent and comely for them that are escaped of Israel" (Isaiah 4:2).

Who is the branch being spoken of here? All through the Old Testament, the branch that is mentioned as coming forth is none other than Jesus Christ, the Lord of glory.

According to Isaiah, there will be a church to whom He will appear beautiful and glorious, excellent and comely. Their motive toward Him will not be one of simply having a reproach removed. No—they will be passionately in love with a Man whom they see as desirous, glorious, excellent!

Right now, there is on the earth a remnant church that desires nothing but Christ. This remnant is but a small portion, perhaps a tenth, of what we think of as the church. I don't believe that the church which will please God in these last days has to be one of multiple thousands of believers. On the contrary, much of what we see taking place in megachurches today does not represent God's heart at all.

No—the heart of the Lord is in those churches where Jesus is the center of attraction—where everything is based upon the preaching of the Cross and built around the presence and character of Christ. God's heart is revealed to those churches that are in love with His Son—where people focus their all on Him!

These are the ones Isaiah refers to as being **"...escaped of Israel"** (same verse). He says of them: **"When the Lord shall have washed away the filth of the daughters of Zion, and shall have purged the blood of Jerusalem from the midst thereof by the spirit of judgment, and by the spirit of burning"** (verse 4).

God has sent His Spirit into the world in these last days to reprove of sin and ungodliness. Many who hear His burning, judging, convicting Word will flee into Babylon—that is, into worldliness—and will be carried away into bondage.

Only a remnant will remain. And Isaiah is saying here that God will bring these few through **"...the spirit of judgment, and...the spirit of burning"** (same verse).

Indeed, the last-day church that will be filled with God's glory is more than just a forgiven church. It is a holy church—one that has been purged by the consuming fire of God's convicting Word. Holiness and purity characterize its people. Isaiah adds, **"...left in Zion...shall be called holy, even every one that is written among the living in Jerusalem"** (verse 3).

You may say, "But, Brother Dave, it's clear this refers only to ancient Israel. Jerusalem and Zion are named here—and that pinpoints this prophecy to the Jewish population of Jerusalem at a certain time in history."

No! It is much more than that. Consider what the Bible says elsewhere: **"But Jerusalem which is above is free, which is the mother of us all"** (Galatians 4:26). **"But ye are come unto mount Sion, and unto the city of the living God, the heavenly Jerusalem, and to an innumerable company of angels"** (Hebrews 12:22).

There is a new, heavenly Jerusalem—a spiritual city that is the mother of all believers: **"...the city of my God, which is new Jerusalem, which cometh down out of heaven from my God..."** (Revelation 3:12). This is what the prophet Isaiah is talking about—a heavenly-minded remnant whom the Lord will bring through His consuming fire!

You see, when you believe on the Lord Jesus Christ, you are born into Zion. Your name is recorded there. And those who have fully given their heart to Jesus—who are intimate with Him and belong to Him—are known in Zion as sons and daughters of God.

The best evidence here that Isaiah is referring to the last-days' church is found in verse 5: **"And the Lord will create upon every dwelling place of mount Zion, and upon her assemblies, a cloud and smoke by day, and the shining of a flaming fire by night: for upon all the glory shall be a defense"** (Isaiah

4:5). Isaiah is predicting God will create a new pillar and cloud to cover His people!

Now, we know that when Isaiah prophesied this, the pillar and cloud in the wilderness had already passed away. Obviously, this was something that had yet to be created—a new thing!

The cloud has to do with direction and comfort—with preservation from all evil and terror, and with guidance. This means God's last-days, holy remnant people will have clear direction. They will not be confused. When everything around them is spinning in different directions and falling apart, they will have a cloud and a pillar of fire to lead them!

Israel had but one tabernacle—and they had one cloud and one pillar of fire. But today we all are tabernacles of the Holy Spirit—and God has provided a cloud and a pillar of fire for every one of us. Every individual—and every repentant, holy congregation—has the cloud of the Spirit to lead them by day and a pillar of Spirit-fire to lead them by night.

God is saying, in other words, "I'm going to see you through, no matter what your situation. Even in the worst storm of your life, you'll have clear direction from Me. I will give you a pillar of fire to lead you—as surely as I did Israel in the wilderness!"

Yet right now in America, there is a raging storm of confusion in the church. So many people are confused. There is little discernment—and yet there is much false doctrine, foolishness and flesh.

Our ministry receives calls and letters from people all over the country who say, "What's going on? I can't figure it out. Our pastor is bringing in strange teachings, and it's tearing our church in two. Is this of God or not? Please tell us. We don't know what to believe anymore!"

My son Gary, who pastors a church in Denver, called me recently. He said, "Dad, I went to a meeting recently where things just went crazy. It almost frightened the leaders. They had to get up and say, 'All right, let's bring this all back to Jesus.'

"At the beginning they'd said it was a move of the Holy Ghost. But then they had to say, 'Let's bring it all back to Jesus.' Well, where had they been, if they had to bring everything back to Jesus?"

Beloved, this kind of thing is frightening. The focus in that meeting never should have been anywhere but on Jesus!

Often people come to me and say, "Brother Wilkerson, you've got to go with us. A great revival has broken out in such-and-such a church. It's marvelous. People are falling down left and right."

Now, I'm not against manifestations. I worked for five years with Kathryn Kuhlman, and I saw people in her meetings fall under the power of the Holy Ghost in a way that was absolutely awesome. There was no manipulation involved; it was a genuine work of the Spirit.

But if people want to tell me a great move of God is going on somewhere today, my first question will be: "Is God's Word being preached there with consuming fire? Are people falling under conviction for sin? Is the cry of the people there for the purging of the spirit of this world?

"Is holiness the result? Is there a strong message of reproof? Does it drive people to Jesus? Does everything focus on Him? Is Christ the sum of it all? Is there a new compassion for lost souls? Are hardened sinners repenting?"

That is the work of the Holy Ghost! He comes to reprove the world of sin, righteousness and judgment. So, if you're going to tell me the Holy Ghost has come down, then these things had better be happening. If not, then judge it for what it is—flesh!

The Holy Remnant Church Is Led Completely by the Holy Spirit!

The Lord has a people in these confusing times who are not confused. They are so given to Jesus—so in love with Him, so open to the reproof of His Spirit, so separated from the wickedness of this age—that they know the ways and workings of the Holy Spirit. They know what is pure and holy, and what is fleshly and foolish. Wherever the cloud moves, they follow!

"...for upon all the glory shall be a defense" (verse 5). The original Hebrew here reads: "Over all shall be a covering of glory." This means, in essence, "Over each of these remnant people, and all of these holy remnant assemblies, there will be a hiding place, a blanket, a covering. And that covering is the glory of God!"

You may remember from Exodus 40 that a cloud of glory covered the tabernacle in the wilderness: **"Then a cloud covered the tent of the congregation, and the glory of the Lord filled the tabernacle. And Moses was not able to enter into the tent of the congregation, because the cloud abode thereon, and the glory of the Lord filled the tabernacle"** (Exodus 40:34-35).

Read also what happened in Solomon's tabernacle, when he dedicated the temple: **"Now when Solomon had made an end of praying, the fire came down from heaven, and consumed the burnt offering and the sacrifices; and the glory of the Lord filled the house. And the priests could not enter into the house of the Lord, because the glory of the Lord had filled the Lord's house"** (2 Chronicles 7:1-2).

Beloved, every time the tabernacle was in order—every time it was completed and prepared according to God's design—His glory came down and filled it.

Now, here in Isaiah 4, we are promised that in the last days the Lord will create a glory that covers His remnant church. The very glory of God is going to fill every heart and cover every house. We will worship under the canopy of God's glory!

What is this glory? It is none other than the manifested presence of Jesus Christ, God's Son! Jesus is the fullness of the Father's glory.

"In that day shall the branch of the Lord be beautiful and glorious..." (Isaiah 4:2). **"...his Son...being the brightness of his glory..."** (Hebrews 1:2-3). The glory can't get any brighter than Christ manifesting Himself to you!

The word *manifested* means "to lay hold of by the hand." In other words, when Jesus' presence fills a place, it is so real, so evident, that your spiritual hands can touch it, your spiritual eyes can see it. It is as real as the air you breathe!

The kind of revival I want to see is the kind where the presence of Jesus becomes so powerful and overwhelming—so beautiful and glorious—that the "fruit" (or, conversions) will be excellent! (see Isaiah 4:2). Already we've seen the beginnings of this in our services at Times Square Church—with people streaming forward, weeping and being broken before the Lord.

If people are going to fall down, I want to see them falling under the conviction of the Holy Ghost. And the vision I want them to receive is a renewed vision of Jesus. And the manifestation I want them to have is their rising from the floor as a new creature in Christ!

That's when people ought to be able to laugh. When the consuming fire has done its purging work, and all sin is gone, and there has been a heartrending—then we should be able to laugh all night long. Let the joy of the Lord come then!

I would not want to attend a church where the glory of God has departed. The psalmist testifies that when the ark was captured by the Philistines, **"(God) delivered his strength into captivity, and his glory into the enemy's hand"** (Psalm 78:61). When the priest Eli's daughter-in law gave birth, her son was named Ichabod, meaning **"...the glory [of the Lord] is departed..."** (1 Samuel 4:21).

Our testimony should be, "If I can't have the presence of Jesus, I don't want to live. He has to be my guide, my cloud, my pillar of fire!"

Why Is the Glory of God so Important Today? What Purpose Is the Glory of His Presence?

The answer is found in Isaiah 4: **"And there shall be a tabernacle for a shadow in the daytime from the heat, and for a place of refuge, and for a covert from storm and from rain"** (Isaiah 4:6).

First, the glory of God's presence will be our shelter from the heat. The Hebrew word for heat means "drought, desolation, barrenness." It is a type of God's judgment on an evil society.

In Revelation 16, the fourth angel of judgment is given

power **"...to scorch men with fire. And men were scorched with great heat, and blasphemed the name of God..."** (Revelation 16:8-9).

Right now, God is turning up the heat. And it is going to get even hotter, with judgments on all sides. But the glory of God will be our cover! **"And there shall be a tabernacle for a shadow in the daytime from the heat..."** (Isaiah 4:6). We won't feel the heat! Instead we'll rest in the cool shadow of Jesus' wings.

Second, the glory of God is our defense, our covering: **"...and for a place of refuge, and for a covert from storm and from rain"** (verse 6). Already we are seeing the rain—not just of Holy Spirit outpourings, but of God's judgments. The storm clouds are gathering—but, thank God, there will be a covering over His holy remnant church!

Perhaps you are saying, "I have no 'glory church' I can attend. All I can find are man-centered churches. Where is my covering from the heat and storm?"

Your dwelling place is the glory of God in your own heart! If Jesus is present in you, manifesting Himself to you, then you are covered in full. If you turn your heart and eyes on Him—allowing God's Word to reprove, convict and correct you—He will manifest Himself to you. He has promised it!

"He that hath my commandments, and keepeth them, he it is that loveth me: and he that loveth me shall be loved of my Father, and I will love him, and will manifest myself to him" (John 14:21).

God says, "I will be there with you. It doesn't matter how bad it gets—I'm going to see you through. I will never leave you nor forsake you!" Amen!

—David Wilkerson was the founding pastor of Times Square Church in New York City. There he ministered to gang members and drug addicts. In 1971, he founded World Challenge, Inc., which supports missionaries and outreaches throughout the world. He died in 2011.

Reprinted by permission: World Challenge, Inc., PO Box 260, Lindale, TX 75771.

EYE HATH NOT SEEN NOR EAR HEARD...

by U.S. Grant

It has been said, and rightly so, that one should never speak of the death and burial of Jesus unless he speaks also of His resurrection (I Cor. 15:1-4).

His death is very necessary to our faith, for "...Without shedding of blood is no remission" for sin (Heb. 9:22). Over 4,000 years ago, God revealed that truth to Moses when He said, "...The life of the flesh is in the blood: and I have given it to you upon the altar to make an atonement for your souls..." (Lev. 17:11). Christ had to be made a sacrifice upon the altar. His resurrection is vitally necessary; for had He not been raised from the dead, He would have been no more than an ordinary man.

When Christ ascended into heaven, something happened which had never happened before: Christ, as glorified humanity, took His place at the right hand of the Father in heaven. Secondly, Christ ascended in order that you and I might receive the blessed infilling of the Holy Spirit. "...If I go not away, the Comforter will not come unto you; but if I depart, I will send him unto you" (John 16:7). Thirdly, Jesus is in heaven at the right hand of God as our Intercessor. "For there is one God, and one mediator between God and men, the man Christ Jesus; Who gave himself a ransom for all, to be testified in due time" (I Tim. 2:5, 6).

Then we have the wonderful promise of Christ's second coming. Thank God He didn't just come once and go away and forget about us. When the disciples stood out on the mountain that day and watched Jesus ascend in a cloud, angels stood by and said, "...Ye men of Galilee, why stand ye gazing up into heaven? This same Jesus...shall so come in like manner as ye have seen him go into heaven" (Acts 1:11).

None of us wants to die until his time comes; but the Scripture says that the dead in Christ will rise first; and "Then we which are alive and remain shall be caught up together with the Lord..." (I Thess. 4:17). Christians believe Jesus is coming back again.

The late President Franklin D. Roosevelt was asked on an occasion: "Mr. President, which do you consider the most important facet of the Federal Government? Is it the legislative, the judicial or the executive?" Mr. Roosevelt replied, "Which do you consider the most important leg on a three-legged stool?" Likewise, if one of these truths is removed from our faith, there will be an imbalance.

There are two vital truths which make Christianity unique and uphold its authenticity. The first truth is the virgin birth. The virgin birth is absolutely essential to the Christian faith (Luke 1:30-35). There is a law of life which points up something very wonderful and precious. A mother carries her unborn child beneath her heart where it is constantly nourished; but not one drop of the mother's blood gets into the veins of the child. Why? Because the blood of the child is supplied solely by the male parent.

If Jesus had been born of an earthly father, His blood would have been contaminated by sin, as our own blood; but He wasn't born of an earthly father. God is His Father. He received God's pure blood into His mortal veins—that blood is divine; it is incorruptible; it is precious. Because there is nothing else in all the universe which will atone for sin other than the blood of Jesus.

Many years ago in India, there was a plague resulting from the Cobra snake bite which was killing many people. No anecdote had been found for the poisonous venom. Feverishly, scientists began accelerating their research techniques. They injected cobra venom into every type of animal, large and small; and inevitably each died. Then they came upon a unique strain of Arabian stallion whose blood could be used as an antidote for the cobra venom.

Jesus Christ took the sting of death in His own body; and His blood is the antidote for sin, for us. That's what makes our faith unique!

The other truth which makes Christianity unique is the truth of the resurrection. The resurrection brings new hope and new life to those who trust in Christ (Rom. 1:3, 4). The resurrection of Christ puts God's seal upon Him as the very Son of God with power both in heaven and on earth!

A young Frenchman once decided he could improve upon the New Testament. He retired and set himself to write a new gospel. When he had finished it, he took it to an old saint in Paris and said, "Look, I've written a new gospel. Would you read it and give me your opinion?" The old Frenchman agreed, and after reading the young man's "gospel" he said, "It's a masterpiece; well done." The young man asked, "Do you think people will accept it?" Thoughtfully, the old saint replied, "Yes, my son, if you will do these things: Teach this gospel, live by it, get yourself crucified for it, get yourself raised from the dead! Then people will accept your new gospel."

When God reached into the corridors of death He didn't bring out Mohammed or Buddha or any other mortal man who claimed to be God's representative. He brought again His beloved Son; and He said, *This is My High Priest forever, after the order of Melchizedek.* The resurrection gave authenticity to His words.

If Christ is not risen, here are the results: 1) Our preaching is in vain. 2) Your faith is in vain. 3) We are false witnesses. "If Christ be not raised, your faith is vain…" (I Cor. 15:17). I'd hate to think I'm still under the bondage from which I was delivered when I gave my heart and life to Christ. No, He "…according to his abundant mercy hath begotten us again unto a lively hope by the resurrection of Jesus Christ from the dead" (I Pet. 1:3).

The old lion, General Wellington, engaged France's Napoleon at Waterloo. If Napoleon had won that battle, we'd all be speaking French today! Hearing the battle was over, people lined the English Channel waiting for some message. Finally, in the late afternoon, the old bircher came out with his semaphores in his hands; and he signaled out across the channel: WELLINGTON DEFEATED… Then one of the famous channel fogs rolled in, and the scene disappeared from view. Many people went home with their hopes dashed because of the message that Wellington had been defeated. But a few of the faithful ones lingered. When the fog lifted, Wellington was still there; and the message was completed: WELLINGTON DEFEATED… NAPOLEON!! Then there was a great cry of triumph on Britain's side.

When Christ hung on that cross, everybody there saw him die; and nobody's faith survived. The message came forth loud and clear: CHRIST DEFEATED! The clouds came in and the fog rolled in; but three days later the clouds and fog were lifted, and the message was completed: CHRIST DEFEATED…DEATH!

There will be a resurrection day for us! Jesus still bears the marks of the cross in His body, and we who trust in Him are coming forth in resurrection!

—Rev. U.S. Grant pastored one of the Assemblies of God's largest churches for many years in Kansas City, Kansas. Though retired, he is still active in ministry.

Reprinted by permission: Christ for the Nations
CFNI, P.O. Box 769000, Dallas, TX 75376-9000, 800-933-2364

APPENDIX

JESUS AND THE FEAST OF THE PASSOVER

By Zoe Ministries

Historical Background

God instituted the observance of the Feast of Passover to remind His people of His deliverance of them from their bondage in Egypt. He sent terrible plagues against Egypt as He tried to convince Pharaoh to let the Israelites go. Pharaoh refused and God sent the tenth and final plague, which was the death of the firstborn of every family in Egypt.

In **Exodus 12:1–14, 43–48** God gave His people instructions on how to be saved from this death. His instructions were as follows:

1. On the tenth day of the month of Nisan every man was to select a male lamb without spot or blemish.
2. He was to observe this lamb for five days to make sure there was nothing wrong with it.
3. On the fourteenth day of Nisan at twilight he was to bring the lamb to his doorstep and kill it, catching some of its blood in a basin.
4. He was to sprinkle the blood on both sides of the door post and above the door post.
5. His family was to enter their house through the blood-stained door and remain there so that they would be protected from the plague of death.
6. They were to roast the lamb on a spit shaped like a crossbar, being careful not to break any of its bones.
7. They were to eat the whole lamb, not leaving any of it until the next day.
8. No uncircumcised person could eat the Passover meal. Only people who accepted the Hebrew God as the one true God and who were in covenant with Him could celebrate this feast.
9. As the Israelites ate this meal, God allowed the angel of death to go throughout the land and kill the firstborn of every house not sprinkled with the blood of a lamb. If the entrance of a house was covered by blood, the angel of death could not enter but had to pass over that house.

In Jesus' day people brought their lambs to Jerusalem or they purchased Temple lambs for sacrifice. In the year Jesus died, about 256,000 lambs were killed in Jerusalem. With this many lambs, it was necessary for the Jews to prepare them for sacrifice at nine o'clock a.m. on the fourteenth of Nisan. They then killed them at three o'clock so the Passover could be completed by six o'clock p.m., the beginning of the next day.

Jesus' Fulfillment of the Requirements of the Feast of Passover

In **Isaiah 53** the prophet predicted that a human "lamb" would give his life in order to deal with the problem of sin and death once and for all. The prophet John the Baptist said of Jesus, **"Look, the lamb of God, who takes away the sin of the world!" John 1:29**. In fulfillment of the Feast of Passover and Isaiah's prophecy in **Isaiah 53,** Jesus **"was oppressed and afflicted, yet He did not open His mouth; he was led like a lamb to the slaughter" verse 7.**

Jesus was set aside to be examined and sacrificed on the exact month, day and hour that Jews were handling their Passover lambs.

1. Jesus entered Jerusalem on the tenth day of the month of Nisan to be set aside as the human "lamb" **(John 12:1, 12–13).**
2. Jesus was observed and tested for five days by the religious leaders. They questioned His authority and asked Him trick questions, hoping He would give a wrong answer they could use against Him. They could not find anything wrong with Him. Even Pilate, after interrogating Jesus, said, **"...I find no fault in him" John 19:4; Matthew 21:23–27; 22:15–46.**
3. Jesus was crucified on the fourteenth day of the month of Nisan. He was nailed on a cross at nine o'clock a.m., the third hour by Jewish time **(Mark 15:25).**
4. At three o'clock (the ninth hour) Jesus died **(Mark 15:33–37).**
5. Jesus' bones were not broken. When the soldiers came to break His legs to hasten His death, they found He had already died **(John 19:31–33).**
6. The Jews hurriedly took Jesus' body down before the Sabbath began at twilight, so He was not left on the cross the next day. Jesus gave His all on the fourteenth of Nisan as the final Passover sacrifice **(John 19:31).**

Personal Application

The Feast of the Passover reminds us today of how God has delivered each of us from bondage to sin and death.

Even though we deserve death as a penalty of our sin **(Romans 3:23; 6:23)**, God made a way for us to be saved. Jesus' blood cleanses us from all sin **(1 John 1:7)**. When we apply Jesus' blood to the doorpost of our heart, death cannot hold us. We no longer need to fear death because the resurrection of Jesus has taken away its sting **(1 Corinthians 15:51–57).**

We are reconciled to God when we acknowledge Jesus as our substitutionary sacrifice **(Ephesians 2:13).** This is the first step in knowing God and walking with Him. Only those who recognized the Hebrew God as their own God could celebrate the Passover feast. When we accept Jesus as our personal Lord and Savior, we come into covenant with God and can enjoy the blessings that come with knowing Him. We can come into God's presence only by being covered by Jesus' blood.

A summary of pages 18–28 of Richard Booker's *Jesus in the Feasts of Israel,* Bridge Publishing, Inc., South Plainfield, New Jersey, 1987. Used by permission from author.

ZOE COURSE DESCRIPTIONS

"My sheep <u>hear</u> My voice, and I <u>know</u> them, and they <u>follow</u> Me." John 10:27 (KJV)

HEARING COURSES

Hearing God's Voice

In this course, everyone is encouraged to participate by applying the principles they read in scripture in order to learn to recognize when the Holy Spirit is speaking. The inner knowing, inner voice, and the authoritative voice of the Holy Spirit are discussed, as well as other manifestations of the Holy Spirit. The Lord is personal and unique, and desires to communicate with each one of His sheep in a personal and unique manner! (This course is a prerequisite for all the following courses except for *How to Hear God's Voice—In Marriage.*)

How To Hear God's Voice—In Christ

In the Hearing God's Voice course we learned how to hear God as individuals, whereas in the In Christ course, we learn how the body of Christ operates together under His direction and to His glory. We look at Romans 12 and examine the motive gifts that determine our individual bents. This study enables us to understand, appreciate and love each other. We also look at the Trinity and how they operate together. We learn about the precious person of the Holy Spirit and how He teaches, guides and comforts us. We also learn about the gifts of the Holy Spirit in 1 Corinthians 12 and 14 brought about as the Holy Spirit moves through us. Participants have remarked that this course has enabled them to see people the way God sees them and how they fit in the body of Christ.

How To Hear God's Voice—In Marriage

This course is based on the love relationship God had with mankind in the very beginning. We examine our attitudes toward each other and how they reflect the greatest love of all, the love of Christ. Do we love and honor each other with the unconditional love that our Lord Jesus had for us while dying on the cross? As in previous classes, we examine scripture, seek the Lord, and ask Him, "How can I better serve and love my spouse?" We discover how we complete each other, not compete with each other.

How To Hear God's Voice—In the Family

In today's society we see the growing deterioration of the family. Parents are confused about what the Bible teaches on family issues. During this course we examine scriptures and what it means to: "Train up a child [early childhood] in the way he should go [and in keeping with his individual bent], and when he is old [teen years can be the best] he will not depart from it." (Proverbs 22:6 AMP with additions)

KNOWING COURSES

How To Know God's Voice—In Intimate Friendship

Intimate Friendship with God! Can we experience such a relationship with the Creator of the universe? Here we examine what the Bible teaches us about the fear of the Lord, and how we can, indeed, have a deeper, more intimate relationship with Him. This is a very personal, yet freeing course on growing intimacy with God.

How To Know God's Voice—In Worship

The focus of this course is on ministering to the Lord. During our time together the Lord draws us corporately into His presence as we worship Him. We study what worship is, why we worship, and how we worship.

How To Know God's Voice—In His Presence

The Lord is calling each one of His sheep to come into His presence and to know Him in a deeper way. This course is not for the new believer nor the faint in heart. Those who are serious about knowing the Father in a more intimate way will find this class challenging but rewarding. Examining Jesus' last days on earth will direct us into the presence of the Lord. This class is for those who have completed other ZOE classes.

How To Know God's Voice—In the Coming of the Lord

Many are proclaiming dates and times when the Lord Jesus will return for His bride. This class is designed to focus on our preparation for His coming, not when He is coming, and to better understand the Lord's statement of Revelation 22:20: "Yes, I am coming." It is the goal of this course to prepare ourselves as the bride of Christ, with hearts that will respond with "Amen. Come, Lord Jesus."

FOLLOWING COURSES

How To Know God's Voice—In His Presence

Evangelism is often thought of as a bad word! In this course we come to realize that God has a special plan for evangelism for us if we are only sensitive and obedient to His voice. Preparing your testimony, leading someone in salvation, and discipling others are a few of the topics discussed in this course. This is a real life-changer as we minister in "power evangelism!"

How To Know God's Voice—In Healing

During this course we examine the scriptures in which Jesus healed the sick. The Holy Spirit highlights these passages as we study, and our faith increases! We realize that Jesus is the Healer, and we are simply His vessels as we listen to and follow His voice.

How To Know God's Voice—In Intercession

Jesus is in constant intercession (Hebrews 7:25). As we come before Him in worship, intercession is a natural outflow of our relationship with Him. By yielding to the Holy Spirit, our ministry to others through intercession will increase.

How To Know God's Voice—In Spiritual Warfare

As we come to know and recognize who our Lord is, He reveals to us who He is not! The tactics of Satan and our spiritual weapons are defined in this class. The Lord leads us in spiritual warfare as He enlists and mobilizes His army!

ONE-ON-ONE DISCIPLESHIP

Discipleship by the Word and the Holy Spirit

This 12-week course was developed by a disciple-maker after many years of successful one-on-one discipleship. Through this method the Holy Spirit is allowed to minister to the disciple through the Word and the encouragement of the disciple-maker. No other techniques or methods are used.

The entire course has been designed to enable individuals to feel confident in making disciples as directed by our Lord: "Therefore go and make disciples of all nations…." Matthew 28:19.

Not only do participants learn what discipleship means according to the Word of God, but they are encouraged to participate in a one-on-one discipleship program as part of the course. This training allows individuals to take great strides in their personal relationship with God and in ministry. It changes lives in a very simple, yet powerful way.

EVANGELISTIC OUTREACH—MINISTRY IN HOMES

Captivated by Their Character

This series of courses called Captivated by Their Character is designed to reach the unbeliever, new believer, and those needing a refresher course on the Trinity.

They are offered in a non-threatening, home atmosphere where every effort is made to make the participant feel comfortable with the material. For example, everyone uses the same Bible, referring to page numbers rather than books, no reading is required outside of the course, and they are given the freedom to express their inadequacies as a believer or non-believer.

The three 6-week courses inside Captivated by Their Character are titled Who Is Jesus?, Who Is God the Father? and Who Is the Holy Spirit?, and are also bound separately.

Additional information is available on the website at www.zoeministires.org/zoe-courses

MAGAZINE LIST

For your convenience we have included the following list of magazines from which this course's articles have been drawn. If you wish to receive these magazines on a regular basis, the subscription information below will help.

Charisma and Christian Life
Subscription Service Department
P.O. Box 420234
Palm Coast, FL 32142-0234

(800) 829-3346
www.charismamag.com

Christ For the Nations
P.O. Box 769000
Dallas, TX 75376-9000

(800) 933-CFNI
www.cfni.org

Decision Magazine
Billy Graham Evangelistic Association
P.O. Box 668886
Charlotte, NC 28266-8886

(877) 247-2426
www.bgea.org

Focus on the Family
Magazines / Subscriptions
Colorado Springs, CO 80995

(800) A-FAMILY (232-6459)
www.family.org

The Last Days Magazine
Last Days Ministries
825 College Blvd., Suite 102, #333
Oceanside, CA 92057

www.lastdaysministries.org

Ministry Today *(formerly **Ministries Today**)*
Magazine Customer Service
600 Rinehart Road
Lake Mary, FL 32746

(407) 333-0600
www.ministrytodaymag.com

Resurrection Fellowship's Newsletter
6502 E. Crossroads Blvd.
Loveland, CO 80538

(303) 667-5479
www.rez.org

Times Square Church Pulpit Series
c/o World Challenge
P.O. Box 260
Lindale, TX 75771

(903) 963-8626
www.worldchallenge.org/en/pulpit_series_newsletter